INTERPRETING GERMAN: ADVANCED LANGUAGE SKILLS

INTERPRETING GERMAN: ADVANCED LANGUAGE SKILLS

• Student Handouts

Ursula Böser and Hugh Keith

Consultant editor: Sarah Butler

Routledge
Taylor & Francis Group

LONDON AND NEW YORK

First published 2001
by Routledge
2 Park Square, Milton Park, Abingdon, Oxon OX14 4RN

Simultaneously published in the USA and Canada
by Routledge
711 Third Avenue, New York, NY 10017

Routledge is an imprint of the Taylor & Francis Group

© 2001 Ursula Böser and Hugh Keith

Typeset in Times and Gill Sans by RefineCatch Limited, Bungay, Suffolk

British Library Cataloguing in Publication Data
A catalogue record for this book is available from the British Library

Library of Congress Cataloging in Publication Data
A catalogue record for this book has been requested

ISBN 978-0-415-24421-3 (student handouts)
ISBN 978-0-415-24420-6 (tutor's book)
ISBN 978-0-415-12562-8 (books and audio)

Printed and bound in Great Britain by TJ International Ltd, Padstow, Cornwall

Contents

Level 3

CD Track List

CD 1

Track 1: Programme Introduction
       2: Level 1. Unit 1. Introduction to the liaison exercise. Dialogue.
       3: Level 1. Unit 3. The use of spelling. Exercise 1. Handout 5.
       4: Unit 3. Exercise 2. Handout 5.
       5: Unit 3. Dialogue.
       6: Level 1. Unit 4. Asking for clarification. Dialogue.
       7: Level 1. Unit 5. Requesting information. Dialogue.
       8: Level 1. Unit 6. Expressing agreement & disagreement. Dialogue 1.
       9: Level 1. Unit 6. Dialogue 2.
     10: Level 2. Unit 7. Note taking. Preparatory Exercise 1. Handout 3.
     11: Level 2. Unit 7 Preparatory exercise 2. Handout 4.

CD 2

Track 1: Level 2. Unit 7. Dialogue
       2: Level 2. Unit 8. Summarising. Preparatory exercise 1. Handout 4.
       3: Level 2. Unit 8. Preparatory exercise 2. Handout 5.
       4: Level 2. Unit 8 Dialogue
       5: Unit 8. Follow-up Exercise 1. Handout 9.
       6: Level 2. Unit 8. Follow-up exercise 2. Handout 9.

CD 3

Track 1: Level 2. Unit 9. Flexibility. Preparatory exercise 2. Handout 6.
       2: Level 2. Unit 9. Dialogue
       3: Level 2. Unit 10. Structuring. Preparatory exercise 1. Handout 6.
       4: Unit 10. Preparatory exercise 2. Handout 7.
       5: Unit 10. Dialogue.
       6: Level 2. Unit 11. Anticipation. Preparatory exercise 2. Handout 6.
       7: Level 2. Unit 11. Handout 7.

CD 4

Track 1: Level 2. Unit 12. Presentation. Preparatory exercise 1. Handout 5.
     2: Unit 12. Preparatory exercise 2. Handout 6.
     3: Unit 12. Dialogue
     4: Level 2. Unit 12. Follow-up exercise 2. Handout 10.

CD 5

Track 1: Level 3. Unit 13. Exposition. Dialogue. Town Planning.
     2: Level 3. Unit 14. Negotiation. Dialogue. Co-determination.
     3: Level 3. Unit 15. Argumentation. Dialogue. Paid & un-paid work.

CD 6

Track 1: Level 3. Unit 16. Negotiation. Dialogue. Computer equipment purchase.
     2: Level 3. Unit 17. Exposition. Dialogue. Education.
     3: Level 3. Unit 18. Argumentation. Dialogue. Traffic Planning.

Level 1 is aimed at individuals with an intermediate knowledge of German grammar and vocabulary such as could be expected from first-year students of German at the start of their studies. It aims to provide a general introduction to the liaison interpreting exercise, the difficulties it poses, and the basic skills and linguistic knowledge it requires. Particular skills such as the ability to memorise and summarise, need to be emphasised from the very beginning, but the main focus at Level 1 is the acquisition and consolidation of the general linguistic knowledge required for successful oral communication. By the end of Level 1, you should have a good grounding in the main speech acts and structuring devices occurring in a range of conversations. By working with the material you should have acquired:

✔ Confidence in your ability to memorise sizeable statements.

✔ The habit of solving problems by anticipation or by 'recycling' vocabulary.

✔ An ability to listen analytically (i.e. listen out for meaning rather than words).

✔ An awareness of the different types of register required for different contexts.

UNIT 1 ···● Background Notes

 INTRODUCTION TO THE LIAISON EXERCISE: DIALOGUE 1

Listen to the recording of Dialogue 1: a conversation between a German student, Gertrud Wieczoreck, and a British one, Peter Mackenzie, who meet during an international conference of student unions in Edinburgh. They are both interested in finding out about each other's university systems. Start by playing the entire conversation without stopping, listening carefully to how the interpreter manages!

When you have done this, play Dialogue 1 again, stopping after each pair of statements and considering the points contained in the following handouts. These are marked with an * in the text.

1a Also, also ich heisse* Gertrud Wieczoreck. Ich studiere in Heidelberg, da bin ich im 4. Semester na ja und jetzt bin ich eben hier, um so ein bisschen zu hören, wie das so in britischen Universitäten ist.

1b Her name is Gertrud Wieschek*. She is in her fourth semester at Heidelberg University and hopes she will find out a lot about British universities here.

POINTS FOR DISCUSSION

1a *Ich heisse*: all conversations involve certain standard speech acts for which you can learn a variety of formulaic expressions both in English and German – greeting somebody, expressing your thanks, asking questions, expressing agreement, disagreement, changing the topic, etc. In this case the two speakers are introducing themselves. If you have the relevant formulations for these at your fingertips in both languages you will have more energy to concentrate on other problems!

Which speech acts might you come across in the following types of conversation?

✔ A debate between two members of opposite political parties on a highly controversial issue.

✔ A journalist interviewing a well-known political personality.

✔ A client who complains to an intransigent airline official about the cancellation of his/her flight.

1b *Gertrud Wieschek*: frequently, spelling is the last resort when dealing with an unknown word in a foreign language. It is a particularly good problem-solving tool for unfamiliar names which often come up during the first part of a conversation if people are not acquainted with each other.

Faced with a somewhat outlandish name the interpreter here settles for the nearest sound that seems familiar – and gets it wrong. It would have been better to ensure accuracy by asking for clarification.

2a Well, hello I am Peter Mackenzie, I am studying in Edinburgh; my subjects* are English and French. I am in my second year and – well what else can I say – well I guess it's nice meeting you and I hope I'll find out a lot about German universities.

2b Er heisst Peter Mackenzie. Er studiert Englisch und Französisch in Edinburg. Er ist im zweiten Jahr und freut sich, dich hier zu treffen. Er hofft, dass er viel Neues über deutsche Universitäten herausfindet.

POINTS FOR DISCUSSION

In 1a and b and 2a and b both speakers make very similar statements in the two languages. During a liaison interpreting exercise you can frequently use the two speakers as 'living dictionaries', noting the way they express things and recycling the phrases at the next opportunity.

2a *subject*: there are other ways of coping with problems. The word that might at first sight pose a problem here is 'subject'. However, the interpreter deals with this efficiently – by avoiding it!

> **3a** Ja also, ich beantworte gerne alle Fragen, schiess halt mal los!
>
> **3b** Well, I'll gladly answer all of your questions* . . . if you have any* . . .

POINTS FOR DISCUSSION

3b *I'll gladly answer*: here, the student interpreter changes from the third to the first person. While there is some disagreement about whether interpreters should use the first or the third person, it is most important to be consistent. For the purpose of this course we shall use the third person – in accordance with common professional practice in interpreting, since it indicates the distance between an interpreted statement and the person who speaks it. (On the other hand – see the note to 6b (Handout 1.7) – it is not necessary to constantly repeat **er/sie sagt dass . . . .**)

if you have any: here the interpreter ends his statement by betraying his insecurity about the meaning of the last turn of phrase in the German. Do not panic if you are faced with a phrase like **schiess halt mal los!** You should always conclude meaning from context. Here the words are just meant to indicate that the speaker is ready to answer questions. How could you put this across?

4a Well, yes of course I have questions, loads of them. To start off with, why don't you tell me a little about the course that you're taking at university? I mean I don't really know what it is you're studying, what your subjects are.

4b Klar hat er viele Fragen*. Zuerst möchte er ein bisschen wissen über dein Studium. Er weiss nämlich gar nicht, was du eigentlich studierst.

POINTS FOR DISCUSSION

4b ***Klar hat er viele Fragen***: note the very appropriate use of register here, as this is a fairly informal conversation. Choice of register depends crucially on context. You would formulate such a statement rather differently if, for example, you were a journalist interviewing a famous politician.

Well naturally there are a number of questions that spring to mind . . .

Ja selbstverständlich fallen mir da sofort einige Fragen ein . . .

5a Ja, Entschuldigung, das hätte ich gleich sagen sollen. Ich studiere Deutsch, also Germanistik und Geographie, das sind also zuerst mal meine Fächer. Der Studiengang dauert rund 6 Jahre, im 4. Semester macht man in der Regel eine Zwischenprüfung, na das ist, genau wie das Wort sagt, eine Prüfung, wenn die Hälfte des Studiums rum ist. Examen macht man dann nach 6 Jahren.

5b Sorry, she forgot to tell you. She is studying German and Geography. After six years you're ready for your finals and halfway through those six years you normally do what is referred to as the 'Zwischenprüfung', an intermediate exam.

POINTS FOR DISCUSSION

5a This is the longest statement so far, but the student interpreter is quite undaunted and deals very well with it because he has listened out for meaning and realised immediately that there is a great deal of redundant information that he can cut out. What are the units of information in this intervention? Reduced to the keywords they would be something like:

forgot
German and Geography
finals
six years
intermediate exam
three years

Further praise is due to the interpreter, who has clearly familiarised himself with some concepts that are specific to German university education. This becomes obvious in the translation of the term **Zwischenprüfung**. Such culturally specific terminology is clearly a central aspect of anticipation. Here, the student chooses to repeat the term in German and then provides a generic translation for it. The way you deal with such concepts will vary according to context: sometimes you will find a direct equivalent and sometimes you will have to give an explanation.

You should think about concepts which are typically British – such as 'fish and chips', 'bed and breakfast', 'The Proms', 'The Labour Party'. What would you do with these if you were dealing with a German speaker who had only a slight knowledge of British culture?

6a OK, six years that's a long time! You mention exams. What kind of exams are they?

6b Peter sagt*, dass 6 Jahre ja eine lange Zeit sei. Er sagt auch, du hättest Examen erwähnt und er möchte wissen, wie die aussehen.

POINTS FOR DISCUSSION

6b The interpreter has to make it clear at all times that s/he is speaking for somebody else, but there is no need to create grammatical problems for yourself! Nowadays even native Germans find indirect speech difficult to master, so it is far better to make life easy for yourself by using direct speech and launching straight into the statement. The above interpretation should be rephrased accordingly:

Sechs Jahre sind ja eine lange Zeit! Du hast Examen erwähnt – wie sehen sie aus?

7a Na ja, diese* Zwischenprüfung und die Abschlussprüfung, das sind mündliche und schriftliche Prüfungen. Daneben gibt es Klausuren am Semesterende, und bei uns auch sehr viele schriftliche Hausarbeiten, also Referate.

7b The intermediate exam she mentioned earlier and the final exams are both written and oral exams. Apart from that, there are end-of-semester tests and they have a lot of essays to write.

POINTS FOR DISCUSSION

7b This is a very good interpretation, which picks up the demonstrative pronoun **diese** as indicating a prior reference and translating it as 'she mentioned earlier'. It is easy to forget that with this kind of conversational situation listeners hear the answers to their questions with a considerable time lag and can therefore at times get confused about references such as **diese, das, es** that come without any details as to what precisely they are referring to. It is therefore sometimes necessary to be particularly clear and even more explicit than the two speakers themselves.

8a Interesting! I'd love to ask more, but it's 4 o'clock already and I think I am right in saying that we both have a workshop we want to go to at 4.15 p.m. So maybe we can continue this conversation tomorrow? Just now I'd like to thank you* and say good-bye.

8b Das ist interessant und er würde gern mehr fragen, aber ihr wollt* beide zu einem Workshop, der gleich anfängt. Vielleicht könnt ihr ja dieses Gespräch morgen fortsetzen? Inzwischen möchte er sich bedanken für die Unterhaltung und sich verabschieden.

POINTS FOR DISCUSSION

8a *I'd like to thank you*: as the conversation concludes, highly formulaic language comes into play again. As with the speech acts at the beginning, it is helpful to have a couple of synonymous versions up your sleeve. What alternatives are there to the interpretation provided on tape?

8b ***ihr wollt***: note that the interpreter rightly converts the inclusive 'we' into **ihr**. She also focuses on the important information in her interpretation of the times given instead of getting unnecessarily worried about the figures!

9a OK, gerne! Also dann Tschüss bis morgen!

9b Great, so see you tomorrow!

 **EXERCISE I**

Listen to the dialogue and try to find at least two alternative ways of formulating your translation. Use short, simple syntax. Do not consult a dictionary but use words and expressions that you are familiar with to paraphrase statements. Now record yourself rendering the statements in English and German. Assess your recording according to the following criteria. Did you:

✔ Convey all the necessary information?

✔ Speak coherently and fluently?

✔ Use intonation to indicate the required emphasis?

✔ Make it clear that you were speaking on behalf of someone else?

Incidentally, these are the basic criteria to apply to all self-assessment of your work on audio or in pairs with fellow students.

UNIT 2 • Introduction

INTRODUCING AND TAKING LEAVE

This unit covers:

- **Introducing people to one another by name**

- **Identifying people's jobs and positions**

- **Introducing a topic**

- **Responding to the above**

- **Thanking and taking leave**

Unless the two speakers have already met, they are likely to start by introducing themselves to one another and end with one or both of them expressing thanks or saying how much they have enjoyed the conversation.

This unit teaches you to have the right formulations at your fingertips to translate these speech acts efficiently and elegantly in both languages. There is nothing worse than a situation where the smiles on the faces of the two speakers become increasingly glazed as they wait for a stumbling and embarrassed interpreter to complete an introduction or express thanks!

As always, it is a good idea for you to learn several different ways of achieving the same effect. It is also important to be aware of the different nuances of meaning of different phrases, particularly where expressions of thanks are concerned.

As with all the other speech acts in Level 1, the formulations learnt here can also come in useful for your own conversations in German and English!

UNIT 2 ···● General Notes

INTRODUCTIONS

There are two basic options here:

■ you can use the physical context (two people standing/sitting opposite one another) and cut down the verbal formulation to a minimum, gesturing to the person as you introduce him/her:

> This is Frau Roth.
>
> Das ist Mr McCutcheon.

■ or you can use a more formal phrase to express what it is that you are doing:

> May I introduce you to Frau Roth?
> May I introduce Frau Roth?
>
> Darf ich Ihnen Mr McCutcheon vorstellen?
> Ich darf Ihnen Mr McCutcheon vorstellen?
> Ich möchte Ihnen Mr McCutcheon vorstellen?

The following phrases are more formal. Just how formal you wish to be will depend on the situation and the status of the speakers:

> Allow me to introduce Frau Roth.
>
> Erlauben Sie mir, Ihnen Mr McCutcheon vorzustellen.

NOTES

1   We have established that the best principle as an interpreter is to use the third person once the conversation has got going. At the beginning, though, the interpreter still has a separate role to play in bringing the two speakers together and introducing them, so it is natural to speak in the first person 'May I introduce Mrs Smith . . .' and, if providing more information about the speakers (see below), to refer to them in the third person 'She is manager of . . .'.

2   It is a good principle not to try to translate people's titles. Refer to German men and women as **Herr X** and **Frau Y** even in English, and English-speaking men and women as 'Mr X', 'Mrs Y', and 'Ms Y' in German. Do not forget the accusative form of **Herr**: **Darf ich Ihnen Herr*n* Schmidt vorstellen?**

3   This may well be the moment when an interpreter has to spell out names. The skill of spelling in German is practised in the next unit!

JOB/POSITION

As well as their name, speakers often give their job or position:

I am a journalist with *The Times*.
I am Managing Director of Newchem Ltd.
I am responsible for public relations in our company.

Ich bin Journalist bei *der Times*.
Ich bin Geschäftsführer von Newchem Ltd.
Ich bin für die PR-Arbeit in unserem Unternehmen zuständig.

NOTES

1   Remember to use the feminine form of functions if you are referring to a woman, **sie ist Journalistin**; **sie ist Geschäftsführerin**.

2   Newspapers have different grammatical genders in German according to their name: **der Guardian**, **die Times**, **der Independent**.

3   In these phrases, 'with' in English is usually translated as **bei** in German:

      Journalist *bei* der Times
      Leiter der PR-Abteilung *bei* Newchem
      Berater *bei* Volkswagen
  but Lehrerin *in* einem Gymnasium

UNIT 2 ....● General Notes

TOPIC FOR DISCUSSION

Unless it is obvious from the context, it may be necessary to explain to one speaker what the other speaker wishes to discuss with him/her:

> Frau Hubert would like to ask you a few questions about your company.
> Professor Smith is interested in discussing the question of university reforms with you.
> Dr. Schnellinger would like to talk to you about the possibility of a student exchange.
> Frau Kästmann would like to talk to you about tomorrow's meeting.
> Mr Busby would like to look round your factory.
>
> Frau Hubert möchte Ihnen (gerne) ein paar Fragen über Ihre Firma stellen.
> Professor Smith würde gerne mit Ihnen (über) das Thema Universitätsreform diskutieren.
> Herr Dr. Schnellinger möchte sich gerne mit Ihnen über die Möglichkeit eines Studentenaustausches unterhalten.
> Frau Kästmann möchte gerne mit Ihnen die morgige Sitzung besprechen.
> Herr Busby würde gerne Ihren Betrieb besichtigen.

Or, in a more day-to-day context like a hotel reception:

> Herr Falkenstein has got a problem/a question/a request.
>
> Herr Falkenstein hat ein Problem/eine Frage/eine Bitte.

NOTES

1   Constructions with **sich unterhalten** require care – do not forget the **sich** and make sure you put it in the right place!

2   Again, it is useful to learn a number of expressions for this speech act, but the precise grammatical construction for each one requires careful practice. The various constructions (which are used in Exercise 1) are as follows:

jemandem Fragen über etwas stellen
sich mit jemandem über etwas unterhalten
etwas mit jemandem besprechen
mit jemandem etwas diskutieren/über etwas diskutieren

RESPONSE

Any suggestion as to what a speaker would like to discuss is bound to evoke some sort of polite response:

Well I'm glad to meet you.
My name is ——— I am ———
I'd be glad to answer your questions/discuss the subject with you/show you round.

Ich freue mich, Sie kennenzulernen.
Mein Name ist ——— Ich bin/arbeite als ———
Ich werde Ihre Frage gerne beantworten/gerne mit Ihnen über das Thema sprechen/gerne einen Rundgang mit Ihnen machen.

TAKING LEAVE

The time has to come when one or other of the speakers has had enough and wishes to end the conversation. Unless the discussion has been particularly acrimonious it is likely that s/he will do this elegantly, with expressions of thanks:

> Those are all the questions he has – thank you very much for answering them.
> Er hat keine Fragen mehr – vielen Dank für Ihre Zeit.
>
> He is most grateful to you for finding time to discuss these matters with him.
> Er ist Ihnen sehr dankbar, dass Sie sich die Zeit genommen haben, dieses Thema mit ihm zu diskutieren.
>
> Thank you very much – he found this a most interesting conversation/discussion/tour.
> Vielen Dank: das war ein sehr interessantes Gespräch/eine sehr interessante Diskussion/ein sehr interessanter Rundgang.
>
> Thank you very much – you've been most helpful.
> Herzlichen Dank – das war sehr hilfreich.

Or even just:

> Thank you very much.
>
> Vielen Dank/herzlichen Dank/er bedankt sich/er dankt Ihnen.

NOTES

1 Note the reflexive construction in:

   sich die Zeit nehmen, etwas zu tun

2 Note the different constructions in:

   er dankt Ihnen für das Gespräch
   er bedankt sich (bei Ihnen) für das Gespräch

UNIT 2

EXERCISE I

This is an exercise to practise the constructions found in Handout 2.4.

Using the phrases below, make up sentences expressing interest in talking to somebody on the subject concerned. Do not move on to Exercise 2 (Handout 2.8) until you are sure you can deliver the statements in Exercise 1 fluently and without hesitation!

Note, always use **gerne** and watch the word order!

Example: Fragen stellen   Ihre Arbeit
            Ich möchte Ihnen gerne ein paar Fragen über Ihre Arbeit stellen.

I   Fragen stellen   das Universitätssystem in Ihrem Land

2   besichtigen   Ihre Abteilung

3   diskutieren   den neuesten Bericht aus Österreich

4   etwas erfahren   Asylgesetze in Grossbritannien

5   besprechen   die gestrige Entscheidung des Ausschusses

6   sich unterhalten   die Situation der Umwelt in Europa

7   ansehen   Produktionsabteilung in Ihrer Firma

8   sich informieren   Kulturpolitik, die in Amerika betrieben wird

9   sich unterhalten   Reaktion auf unseren Vorschlag
        (mit Ihnen und Ihren Kolleginnen)

10 etwas erfahren   Ihre Einstellung zur Einführung von Studiengebühren in
                                            Grossbritannien

EXERCISE 2

This second exercise now practises the full process of introducing a person and establishing the topic to be discussed. Work in pairs, with one of you introducing the people formally in German and stating what they would like to talk about, and the other person producing a polite response. Use the English notes below to provide the content of what you say:

1   Jasmine Bunce, journalist with *The Times*. Ms Bunce is eager to ask the German speaker a few questions about the unemployment situation in Germany.

2   Henry Proctor, Managing Director of Northern Recyclers Ltd. Mr Proctor is interested in talking to the German speaker about the possibility of cooperating with his company.

3   Mary Forbes, Director of Public Relations for Ford Great Britain. Mrs Forbes would like to take a look at the German speaker's factory.

4   Dr Henrietta Fellows works as an advisor for the National Trust. Dr Fellows would like to have a chat about the talk which the German speaker has just given.

5   John Paton is a teacher in a secondary school in Birmingham. He wants to explore the possibility of setting up a school exchange.

6   James Nasmith is a freelance journalist. He has a problem with a translation which the German speaker may be able to solve.

UNIT 2

EXERCISE 3 (PAIR-WORK)

How would you round off the following conversations? Work in pairs – one of you formulating a statement in English and the other putting it into German.

1   A lively and informative discussion about German politics.

2   An interview during which you were asking a German artist about her work.

3   A brief interview with a very busy politician.

4   A tour of a factory.

UNIT 3 ....● Introduction

SPELLING

This unit covers:

■ **How to ask for a word or words to be spelt out**

■ **How to pronounce the letters of the alphabet which are peculiar to German**

■ **How to check that your understanding of the spelling is correct**

ASKING FOR A WORD TO BE SPELT

No interpreter can be expected to cope easily with names which s/he has not come across before. Obviously one does not want to have to ask for every single name mentioned to be spelt out. But if unknown names do crop up, it is a sign of a good interpreter that s/he checks the spelling rather than relying on guesswork!

This is when pen and paper will come in handy!

There are various ways of asking in German, using either **schreiben** or **buchstabieren**:

> Können Sie mir sagen, wie man das schreibt?*
> Wie schreibt man das?
> Wie wird das geschrieben?
> Können Sie das (bitte) buchstabieren?
> Wie buchstabiert man das?

*Note that the first example above exceptionally involves the use of the first person, whereas the other two require the impersonal form using **man** or the passive.

The English phrases are:

> Do you mind spelling that for me?
> Could you spell that for me?
> How does one/do you spell that?
> How do you write that?

If things go too fast you can always say:

> Können Sie das bitte langsamer (*or* noch einmal) buchstabieren?

PRONOUNCING THE LETTERS OF THE ALPHABET

The following consonants in German are likely to cause the biggest problem, as their pronunciation differs markedly from the English:

g (gay)
h (ha)
j (yot)
k (ka)
qu (coo)
v (fow)
w (vay)
y (üpsilon)

Note also: nn, pp, oo = doppel n, doppel p, doppel o.

The vowels can also lead to confusion:

a (aah)
e (ay)
i (eee)
o (o)
u (ooh)

You also occasionally need to be able to identify when a word is spelt with a capital letter – although there is no need to identify every single noun when you are spelling a word to Germans – they (usually) know the rules!

Grand Marnier = grosses Gay, er, ah, en, day
        neues Wort: grosses M, ah, er, en ee, ay, er

In addition to the above, please note the following special characters in German:

ü = u mit Umlaut or ü
ö = o mit Umlaut or ö
ä = a mit Umlaut or ä
ß = scharfes s or eszed*

* The recent reform of German spelling means that this character is liable to disappear from the language in the long term. This course does not use ß.

CHECKING YOUR UNDERSTANDING OF THE SPELLING

Of course, you may not always want to know the full spelling, but merely to check whether your assumptions about how a word is spelt are correct. Or you may also want to check whether a word is written with a capital or small letter at the beginning or with a hyphen. In such cases you can ask questions like:

> Schreibt man Mozartkugel wie der Komponist Mozart und dann k,u,g,e,l?
> Hugo-Wolfstrasse wie der Wolf?
> Wird das mit einem (zwei) M geschrieben?
> Schreibt man das mit Bindestrich?
> Or   Hat Wieczoreck-Zeul einen Bindestrich?
> Ist das *ein* Wort?
> Or   Schreibt man das getrennt oder zusammen?
> Schreibt man das gross oder klein?
> Or   Mit Gross-oder Kleinbuchstaben?

And finally you might want to check back by asking:

> Stimmt das so: . . .?
> Ist das so richtig: . . .?

AUDIO EXERCISE 1

Try spelling the following. Listen to the correct version on the audio and repeat as rapidly as possible:

1	Greyerzer (Gruyère cheese)	6	Thyssen
2	Henshaw	7	Volkswagen
3	Tyningham	8	Thüringen
4	Jamboree	9	Schröder
5	Kilderkin	10	Miscellaneous

 AUDIO EXERCISE 2

Try out your spelling skills on the following addresses:

Siegfried Petzold, 16866 Minnashöh, Lenzwälderstrasse 12a
Schmalz-Jacobson, 04758 Müllenhagen, Im Krähenwinkel 18
Hans-Günther Tietjen, 04603 Windischleuba, Siebenbürgener Weg 182
Mathilde Zywitz, 25821 Breklum, Untere Mühlengasse 21

EXERCISE 3

What questions would come to mind with the following words?

Frau Wieczorek-Zeul
Cannstatt (a part of Stuttgart)
Unterer Weg
Der Meerschaum
Die Pyrenäenhalbinsel

DIALOGUE I

This is your first opportunity to try your hand at interpreting an entire conversation which you have not heard before. The dialogue will require the use of quite a number of the phrases you have learnt in this unit.

SITUATION

You are employed at a campsite near Braemar in Scotland which has received a number of bookings from a German travel agency. The guests are all to arrive on the same day and you have been asked to help with the registration process. People will come equipped with a booking reference number. Names, addresses, car numbers will all have to be conveyed with precision. Do not take a chance in assuming you have got it right – ask back whenever necessary!

Note that the tone of this conversation is fairly colloquial but that the speakers are nevertheless brief and to the point. Try to emulate this with short, succinct sentences which package information in a way that would avoid a lengthy exchange.

Remember, there is a queue of Germans building up at the Braemar campsite!

NOTES ON DIALOGUE I

formalities: **die Formalitäten**. This noun is often used in conjunction with the word **abwickeln** i.e. 'to deal with'. As so often with English words of Latin origin, the German is very similar – though of course pronounced in a different way.

booking reference number: **die Buchungsnummer**.

registration number: here: **die Autonummer**.

cash: **das Bargeld** (versus **der Scheck** or **die Kreditkarte**).

Euroscheck: note that this is pronounced as in **Europa**.

(bank) account: **das Konto**.

brochure: **die Broschüre**.

UNIT 4 ···● Introduction

ASKING FOR CLARIFICATION

This unit covers:

■ **How to ask someone to repeat a phrase or word which you have not heard clearly**

■ **How to ask someone to repeat an abbreviation**

■ **How to ask someone to explain an unfamiliar concept**

■ **How to identify the precise word or phrase which you are asking about**

REQUESTING CLARIFICATION

There will always be occasions when you have to ask back about a word, a concept which you have not understood, or a point which does not seem to make sense. After all, speakers do not necessarily always make their meaning clear – either in English or in German!

You should have no hesitation about asking back for clarification whenever you are in doubt – and you need to be able to do this swiftly and effectively, making clear what precise concept or word requires clarification, at which point in the statement it occurred, and maybe even why you failed to understand it.

A PHRASE NOT HEARD

There may be words or phrases which have not been understood aurally:

> Ich habe das nicht richtig gehört/verstanden. Bitte, können Sie das wiederholen?
>
> I'm afraid I didn't quite catch that – could you repeat it please?

AN UNFAMILIAR WORD

Or a statement may contain a crucial word with which you are unfamiliar:

> Sie haben das Wort 'Fertigungstiefe' verwendet. Was bedeutet das, bitte?
>
> You used the term 'vertical integration' – what does that actually mean?

AN UNKNOWN ABBREVIATION

Or a speaker may use an abbreviation with which you are unfamiliar:

> Wofür steht die Abkürzung BBC/die Abkürzung, die Sie verwendet haben?
>
> What does (the abbreviation) BBC stand for?

continued

AN UNFAMILIAR CONCEPT

Or there may be a concept which you do not understand:

> Was versteht man unter mittelständische Unternehmen?/Was bitte sind mittelständische Unternehmen?
>
> What do you understand by SMEs? Could you define what you mean by SMEs?

IDENTIFYING THE SITE OF THE PROBLEM

Or there may be a need to identify a problem at a particular point in the conversation:

> Sie haben am Anfang/in der Mitte/ am Ende etwas gesagt, was ich nicht verstehe.
> You said something at the start/in the middle/at the end which I don't understand.
>
> Nachdem Sie von 'führenden, Unternehmen' sprachen, haben Sie etwas gesagt, was ich nicht verstehe.
> After you talked about 'major companies' you said something I didn't understand.

You should learn at least two ways of expressing such questions. And remember you are asking a favour of the speaker and should therefore formulate the request politely. The easiest way to do this, of course, is by adding the word '**bitte**' – preferably at the beginning of the request. Other linguistic indicators of politeness such as the use of the subjunctive will be dealt with in later units.

EXERCISE 1

In the following statements in German there are certain words or phrases in italics. Imagine you have not understood these (maybe you have not!), and ask for clarification in the most appropriate manner. In many cases there will be more than one possibility of phrasing your enquiry.

1 Eine der grössten Herausforderung für die deutsche Wirtschaft ist die *Standortfrage*.

2 Die Lohn- und *Lohnnebenkosten* deutscher Unternehmen sind im internationalen Vergleich zu hoch.

3 *Der BDI* hat zum Beispiel festgestellt, dass der Durchschnittslohn in der Automobilindustrie zweimal so hoch ist wie in Frankreich. Und verglichen mit Japan ist er ein Drittel höher.

4 Mit der zunehmenden *Globalisierung der Wirtschaft* verlagern immer mehr deutsche Hersteller ihre Produktion ins Ausland.

5 Es gibt viele Gründe, warum deutsche Löhne so hoch sind. Einer davon ist der von allen Berufstätigen zu bezahlende *Solidaritätszuschlag*.

6 Die *Überalterung* der Gesellschaft ist besonders deutlich in Deutschland zu beobachten.

7 Die *Pflegeversicherung* ist zur Zeit eine sehr umstrittene Angelegenheit in Deutschland.

8 Immer mehr Deutsche nehmen eine *Hypothek* auf, um eine Wohnung zu kaufen.

9 *Seit der Wende* ist die Arbeitslosigkeit in Deutschland sehr stark gestiegen.

10 Die *öffentlich-rechtlichen Fernsehanstalten* sind zunehmend kommerziellem Druck ausgesetzt.

UNIT 4 ....● Background Notes

🎧 DIALOGUE I

For this dialogue, we return to our student conference in Unit 1. Here, we have two people exchanging ideas about student co-determination. A number of abbreviations and concepts will come up in the course of the conversation which you are not likely to know and this will force you to use the linguistic tool kit described in Handout 4.2.

EXERCISE 2

This exercise requires you and a partner to put together a conversation which is a continuation of the one you have just been working on and then to play it through with a third student acting as the interpreter. The notes below give you some ideas for the content, but feel free to vary it as you like. As this is the first time you have done something like this, you may need to spend some time preparing it and do some homework on the terminology used.

NB: remember that you are using an interpreter because you (ostensibly) do not understand the other language being used. Take everything the interpreter says at face value – do not impose meaning on it because of your knowledge of German or English. If necessary tell the interpreter you do not understand.

German student:	What about student grants?
British student:	These are increasingly a thing of the past. Many students with reasonably well-off parents receive no grant at all.
German student:	Grants or loans? In Germany you have to pay back the amount once you start working.
British student:	Same in Great Britain. Controversial – means graduates start life with debts.
German student:	In Germany you only pay back when you get a job, interest-free, and the amounts are relatively low each month.
British student:	Sounds as though the German system is more humane than the British one!

Continue as you think fit, but only write down keywords for your conversation.

Now run through the conversation with your interpreter, recording the performance if possible. Then listen to the recording with the following questions in mind:

✔ Did the interpreter ask back efficiently where this was necessary?

✔ Was the interpretation sufficiently precise or did its questions lead to lengthy interchanges?

✔ Did the interpreter formulate and deliver the questions politely?

✔ Did the interpreter manage the transition between the use of the first and third persons?

UNIT 5

REQUESTING INFORMATION

This unit covers:

■ **How to signal politely that you would like to ask someone for information**

■ **How to ask a direct question using a "W-word"**

■ **How to ask a question using indirect speech**

FORMULATING A REQUEST

In many interpreted conversations the speakers are trying to elicit information from one another. The structure of the conversation may be one-sided – for example, an interview in which a journalist asks questions and the other person merely responds to these. Or there may be an exchange of questions – as when two businesspeople meet for the first time and each tries to find out about the other's company.

In both cases it is important for the interpreter to be able to formulate requests for information in an efficient, elegant – and polite – manner. In both German and English, directly posed questions can sometimes seem rather abrupt – even rude. So both languages use circumlocutions to soften the blow:

> I wonder if you could tell me when you first came to Britain?

or

> May I ask when you first came to Britain?

rather than:

> When did you first come to Britain?

Other formulations in English are:

> Could you perhaps tell me . . .?
> I wonder if you could tell me . . .?
> Perhaps you could tell me . . .?

Equivalent phrases in German are:

> Können Sie mir vielleicht sagen, wann Sie zum ersten Mal nach Grossbritannien gekommen sind?
> Darf ich Sie fragen, wann Sie zum ersten Mal nach Grossbritannien gekommen sind?

Or:

> Vielleicht könnten Sie mir sagen . . .?
> Ich hätte gern gewusst . . .
> Ich hätte Sie gern gefragt . . .

continued

HANDOUT 5.2

(continued)

NOTE

These polite formulations are most useful during the early stages of a conversation, as they signal the approach of a question, thus reducing any potential shock effect which that question may have. Once the conversation is under way and a whole series of questions are being posed (e.g. during an interview) it is not necessary to use these phrases all the time.

Do not forget that all these phrases in German generate subordinate clauses which require a final verb. The following exercise allows you to practise converting direct questions into indirect ones.

Do not forget that questions which do not start with an interrogative word ('when', 'why', 'where', etc.) require the use of **ob** in German when they are formulated indirectly:

Do you have a PR division in your company?

Er möchte gern wissen, *ob* Sie in Ihrem Unternehmen eine PR-Abteilung haben?

EXERCISE I

Formulate the following questions in a more indirect fashion:

1   Wie lang sind Sie schon hier in England?

2   Seit wann arbeiten Sie für Shell?

3   Warum ist die Arbeitslosigkeit in Deutschland immer noch so hoch?

4   Wie oft fahren Sie in die USA?

5   Waren Sie schon mal in Japan?

6   Versuchen Sie auch, Ihre Produktivität zu erhöhen?

7   Was sind die grössten Probeme, die Sie auf diesem Gebiet haben?

8   Warum haben Sie uns nicht früher angerufen?

EXERCISE 2

Ask the following questions directly in German:

1	Have you been to Edinburgh before?
2	How long have you been waiting for me?
3	Would you like to have a look round our factory?
4	Are you satisfied with the quality of our products?
5	What measures would you suggest?
6.	When can we meet again?
7	What are you doing this evening?
8	What is your opinion on this problem?

Now reformulate them in a more indirect, polite manner!

🎧 DIALOGUE I

A German politician, Hermann Filbinger, is visiting Britain and has agreed to give a British journalist, Joan Hancock, an interview about the state of the German economy. Think beforehand about the concepts likely to be mentioned. No discussion of economics in Germany can fail to touch on the topics of recession, unemployment, inflation, European Monetary Union, reunification, etc.

UNIT 5 ....● Vocabulary

NOTES ON DIALOGUE I

Konvergenzkriterien: 'convergence criteria' – the conditions laid down for the economies of member states wishing to join the European Monetary Union.

die neuen Bundesländer: this is a much-used phrase in German nowadays. Perhaps the most useful translation is 'the eastern German states'. Depending on the context, 'Eastern Germany', or: 'the new federal states (in Eastern Germany)' might also do.

die Wende: this refers to an entire historical concept – the period of political change which culminated in the collapse of the GDR and the reunification of Germany. As often as not, though, it is just used loosely to refer to reunification – as is this case here. It can be rendered as 'reunification', 'political change', or even 'the collapse of the GDR' or 'the fall of the Berlin wall', depending on the context.

AGREEMENT AND DISAGREEMENT

This unit covers:

■ **How to express agreement with varying degrees of emphasis**

■ **How to express disagreement with varying degrees of emphasis**

UNIT 6 ··● General Notes

PHRASING AGREEMENT/DISAGREEMENT

In most conversations – particularly discussions rather than interviews – there will be cause for the speakers to agree or disagree with each other. This can be done either explicitly i.e. by stating **Da ist sie anderer Meinung** or **Da stimmt er Ihnen nicht zu**, or it can be stated with less emphasis, by preambling a statement with the turn of phrase **Sie glaubt nicht, dass**.

The important point to remember in this context is that there are different degrees of agreement or disagreement. There is a huge difference between a speaker thinking that something the other person says is totally nonsensical and finding it acceptable with some minor reservations. The precise degree of agreement or disagreement is also likely to have a considerable impact on the further course of a conversation, especially negotiations or an attempt to come to a consensus. It should also be noted that formulations of disagreement in particular are highly context-sensitive, i.e. a greater or lesser degree of diplomacy and caution is required according to who is involved.

Here are some examples of how to agree or disagree and some suggestions of how to increase the forcefulness of such statements:

AGREEMENT

He agrees.
Da stimmt er Ihnen zu.

He agrees with you (on that).
In diesem Punkt stimmt er mit Ihnen überein.

She shares your opinion.
Sie ist auch dieser Meinung.
Sie ist ganz Ihrer Meinung.
Sie teilt diese Meinung.

That is true.
Das stimmt.

It's true that . . .
Es stimmt, dass . . .

Please note that there is an important difference between **übereinstimmen** and **einverstanden sein**. The former expresses agreement with someone's opinion; the latter agreement to a course of action.

DISAGREEMENT

One can simply use negation to express disagreement, i.e.:

> She doesn't agree with you.
> Da stimmt sie Ihnen *nicht* zu.
>
> He doesn't agree with you (on that).
> In diesem Punkt stimmt er *nicht* mit Ihnen überein.
>
> She doesn't agree with you.
> Sie ist *nicht* dieser/Ihrer Meinung/Auffassung.
>
> She doesn't share your opinion.
> Sie teilt Ihre Meinung *nicht*.
>
> That's (certainly) not true.
> Das stimmt *nicht*.
>
> It's not true that . . .
> Es stimmt *nicht*, dass . . .

But there are also other possibilities, such as:

> She doesn't accept that.
> Da muss er Ihnen *widersprechen*.
>
> He is of a different opinion.
> Er ist da *anderer Meinung*.
>
> Or more colloquially:
>
> Herr Santer sees things differently.
> Herr Santer *sieht das anders*.
>
> Or formally:
>
> She cannot agree with you on that.
> Sie kann sich *Ihrer Meinung nicht anschliessen*.

LEVELS OF AGREEMENT/DISAGREEMENT

Also note that there are various ways to step up or tone down the degree of agreement or disagreement, such as:

Agreement:

> *völlig/uneingeschränkt*
> . . . mit Ihnen übereinstimmen/Ihrer Meinung sein/Ihnen zustimmen.
>
> *nicht ganz*
> . . . mit Ihnen übereinstimmen/Ihrer Meinung sein/Ihnen zustimmen.

Disagreement:

> *überhaupt nicht*
> . . . mit Ihnen übereinstimmen/Ihrer Meinung sein/Ihnen zustimmen.
>
> *deutlich widersprechen*
> (or even):
> *ganz deutlich/scharf/schärftstens widersprechen.*

Conversely one might :

> *etwas/ein wenig widersprechen*
> sich Ihrer Meinung nicht *ganz* anschliessen
> *Ihnen nur mit Einschränkungen zustimmen*

EXERCISE I (PAIR-WORK)

Read out the following statements to your partner, who should do a summary translation such as you would provide during a liaison exercise (you are not looking for a polished translation).

You should then give an answer which indicates your own personal view on the matter – with a reason for the agreement or disagreement.

I   The weather in Great Britain is generally very mild and pleasant.

2   The European single currency is to be highly welcomed.

3   The environment is one of the biggest problems in the world today.

4   The break-up of the Soviet Union has brought enormous political problems.

5   Bob Dylan and Mick Jagger have beautiful singing voices.

6   Charlie Chaplin has made some of the best films that have ever been made.

7   People do not need education to be happy.

8   German reunification has proved to be a big problem.

9   German is a very difficult language.

10 Scotland is far more interesting and beautiful than England.

EXERCISE 2

The following statements are highly controversial and as such invite very strong feelings of agreement and disagreement. Using the same method of pair-work as for Exercise 1, start with some lukewarm agreement and disagreement, then step it up.

1	All politicians are liars.
2	Young people are not interested in working nowadays.
3	Students have a very easy life.
4	Cricket is a much better game than football.
5	Capitalism is a better system than communism.
6	The world needs nuclear energy.

🎧 DIALOGUE I

This conversation takes place in a travel agency. A customer has a complaint about a ferry booking made by a London travel agency with branches in Germany. The problem is that there is only one cabin booked for the return journey whereas the customer had wanted two. He therefore goes to the German branch to have the ticket changed and also to complain about the oversight.

UNIT 6 ....● Vocabulary

NOTES ON DIALOGUE I

ferry: **die Fähre**.

branch: **die Zweigstelle**.

to book: **reservieren**.

cabin: **die Kabine**.

return journey: **die Rückfahrt**.

travel agent: **das Reisebüro**.

der Anspruch: 'claim'.

by phone: **übers Telefon** or **telefonisch**.

to be annoyed: **sich ärgern, etwas ärgerlich finden, verärgert sein**.

e-mail: the term **elektronische Post** does exist, but German tends to take on board English computing terms, so **E-mail** is quite acceptable.

impressed: **beeindruckt**.

service: **der Service**.

UNIT 6

🎧 DIALOGUE 2

This is a conversation between two environmentalists. One of them is a German member of Greenpeace, supporting direct action, the other a member of Friends of the Earth with a less forceful stance. They are discussing possible action to oppose the building of roads in areas of great natural beauty. The Greenpeace member defends direct action such as has taken place in Great Britain, whereas the member of Friends of the Earth tends to prefer lobbying.

NOTES ON DIALOGUE 2

study group: here: **die Forschungsgruppe**.

campaign: **Aktion**.

assessment: **die Einschätzung, die Beurteilung**.

areas of great natural beauty: **landschaftlich schöne Gebiete/Regionen**.

gegen ein Gesetz verstossen: 'to commit an offence'.

Member of Parliament: **die/der Parlamentsabgeordnete(r)** – in written texts about Germany they are often referred to as **MdB** i.e. **Mitglied des Bundestags**.

FOLLOW-UP EXERCISE 1

This is a role-play exercise in German. In groups of five, prepare for the following scenario:

A Heidelberg University student society has generated a considerable amount (DM 800) of income through various activities. A number of you meet to decide on how to spend this money. Inevitably there are differences of opinion on the matter. If everybody got what they wanted the society would end up in considerable debt.

Person A wants DM 300 for sports equipment, person B wants DM 450 to fund a trip to London, and person C would like DM 300 to help with a student theatre production. Person D wants to make a donation to the student hardship fund. The discussion is chaired by the president of the student society. S/he will have to achieve a compromise that can be financed. In addition s/he would like to ensure that a small financial reserve is retained.

LEVEL 2 ● Introduction

By the time you undertake Level 2 you will have acquired a basic tool kit of commonly occurring speech acts and should be able to manage a conversation in the way described in Handout 4.2. Note that a degree of overlearning of these is required, since the interpreting situation is always a stressful one – be it in a real life or a classroom setting – and thus formulations which might well be familiar to you will not necessarily trip as easily off the tongue as you might wish.

By the end of this section you should be able to:

- ✓ Take notes which enable you to reproduce relatively lengthy statements.

- ✓ Cope efficiently with utterances that are high in redundancies and repetition.

- ✓ Process statements that are poorly or not very explicitly structured.

- ✓ Avoid problems by displaying a degree of linguistic and syntactic flexibility rather than getting stuck on a literal rendering.

- ✓ Expand successfully where an utterance either assumes intercultural knowledge or has been phrased in an elliptical way.

In addition to focusing on the specific skills required in liaison interpreting, this level will cover subjects with an area studies orientation. The individual skills and topic matters are:

Skill	Subject area
7 Note-taking	Social welfare
8 Summarising	Federalism in Europe
9 Flexibility	EU expansion
10 Structuring	German reunification
11 Anticipation	The environment
12 Presentation	Television

Note that all of these topics will require familiarity with the topic matter discussed. Two essential resources for the preparation of these sessions are the present edition of *Aktuell* (published annually by Harenberg Verlag) and the Internet. An Internet search in the two languages should be a standard form of preparation for each of the dialogues.

continued

HANDOUTS

For Level 2 these contain:

■ **Overview of the skills covered and activities included**

■ **General notes which introduce a particular skill and in some cases associated vocabulary items**

■ **Interpreter's tips i.e. things to bear in mind or to remember (as an addition to some units)**

■ **Preparatory exercises**

■ **Notes on the dialogue**

■ **Background to the dialogue**

NOTE-TAKING

Skills covered in this unit:

■ **Layout of notes**

■ **Development of appropriate abbreviations**

Activities include:

■ **Two preparatory exercises in taking notes from German and English statements**

■ **A dialogue with relatively long exchanges that offers scope for using notes**

APPROPRIATE NOTE-TAKING

Anyone who has seen a conference interpreter in action, reproducing an entire speech several minutes in length, will have marvelled at the apparent ease with which a professional can jot down a few words and symbols and use these as the basis for producing a fluent and accurate account of what the speaker has just said.

Note-taking of this kind is a highly skilled process requiring months if not years of practice. But it is possible to use some of the basic principles involved to develop a useful technique for coping with relatively lengthy statements made during a liaison interpreting session.

It is important to realise, however, that the liaison interpreter's main tool is his or her memory. Any notes that he or she takes are intended merely as an extra aid. Indeed, in many professional situations it is virtually impossible to take notes – think of a factory tour or a conversation between two politicians or business people during a journey.

The introductory chapter on note-taking in this course presents some useful basic principles:

✔ The layout of your notes.

✔ Selecting what points to record.

✔ The importance of linkwords.

✔ The use of abbreviations and symbols.

This unit offers you an opportunity to try implementing some of these strategies. Remember, though, that it will take you time to develop a system that you find useful. And the best tool for recording information is still your short-term memory!

UNIT 7 · ● Activity

 PREPARATORY EXERCISE 1

ENGLISH–GERMAN INTERPRETING

Listen to the statements on the audio, stopping it after each one and writing down a few words to remind you of the contents. Make sure that you adhere to the layout principles described in the introductory chapter to Level 2:

✓ Number the pages of your notebook in advance.

✓ Divide the page into two columns.

✓ Leave a space between individual points.

✓ Use the full width of each column, noting the main points on the left and subsidiary points further across to the right.

✓ Leave a margin for linkwords.

Then restart the audio and reproduce the statement from your notes in German.

Remember that it is the gist of what was said that you have to reproduce – not necessarily the precise formulation. Indeed, you should try to develop the habit of simplifying the language when you note down individual words. Keep your notes short!

When you have finished the exercise, discuss your notes with your fellow students – everyone develops their own, personal system in time, but you can learn from others too!

PREPARATORY EXERCISE 2

GERMAN–ENGLISH INTERPRETING

Listen to the following statements, stopping the audio after each one and writing down a few words to remind you of the contents. Make sure that you adhere to the layout principles described in the introductory chapter to Level 2:

✔ Number the pages of your notebook in advance.

✔ Divide the page into two columns.

✔ Leave a space between individual points.

✔ Use the full width of each column, noting the main points on the left and subsidiary points further across to the right.

✔ Leave a margin for linkwords.

Then restart the audio and reproduce the statement from your notes in English.

Remember that it is the gist of what was said that you have to reproduce – not necessarily the precise formulation. Indeed, you should try to develop the habit of simplifying the language when you note down individual words. Keep your notes short!

When you have finished the exercise, discuss your notes with your fellow students – everyone develops their own, personal system in time, but you can learn from others too!

UNIT 7 ·· ● Background Notes

 DIALOGUE I

This is a conversation between a journalist from a German newspaper and a Mr Rosewell from the Department of Social Security (**Sozialministerium**). Much of the ground covered – and some of the statements – are very close to the material found in the two preparatory exercises, so only a few items of vocabulary have been explained in advance, on the assumption that you will have familiarised yourself with the other terms before you start on the dialogue.

On a couple of occasions you may come up against an idiomatic phrase in English or German – the trick here is to home in on the actual core meaning of the phrase and translate that, rather than trying to find a similarly idiomatic phrase. You will learn more about the importance of such flexibility in Unit 9.

NOTES ON DIALOGUE 1

in . . . need: **bedürftig**.

to look after oneself: **sich selbst zu versorgen**.

verschwenderisch: 'wasteful'.

üppig: 'lavish(ly)'.

training: in the sense of 'training for a job', this is **Ausbildung** or **Berufsausbildung**.

SUMMARISING

Skills covered in this unit:

■ **Identifying primary information**

■ **Eliminating redundancy and repetition**

Activities include:

■ **Two recorded versions of a dialogue on federalism**

■ **Three preparatory exercises requiring combined audio- and group-work**

■ **Three follow-up exercises based on the dialogues. Two of these require you to work on your own; a third involves pair-work**

ELIMINATING REPETITION

All communication involves a degree of repetition and redundancy. Without this we would have considerable difficulty in making sense of what other people are saying.

Sometimes, though, a degree of repetition can also have a communicative function, lending emphasis to what is being said. An example would be a demonstration of pleasure at meeting somebody or a profuse expression of thanks.

However, too much redundancy that does nothing to provide us with further information is at best not helpful and at worst downright boring. Moreover, what might be tolerable from a speaker with whom we communicate directly and who formulates his/her utterances as they go along is not necessarily what is expected from an interpreter. After all, the interpreter has the benefit of hindsight, i.e. s/he has heard and processed a statement in full and is thus not making a spontaneous statement but one which s/he has had some time to plan. A crucial part of this planning consists of deciding whether things can be summarised or even left out, for example because they merely repeat what has been said already or refer to shared knowledge which does not need to be spelt out. In this unit's dialogue we introduce you to two particularly long-winded speakers. Their way of formulating a statement challenges the interpreter to cut through the verbiage and get to the gist of the message!

UNIT 8

Where speakers consistently repeat themselves – as in our dialogue example – you will be able to rely on your memory to a considerable extent.

If you do take notes, resist the temptation to write down redundancies and repetitions. Your notes should reflect the bare structure of a statement. Where a speaker uses a lot of words to say very little, it is the gist of what s/he says which should appear in the notes.

UNIT 8

🎧 PREPARATORY EXERCISE 1

On the audio you will hear some examples of highly redundant German and English. Each statement is followed by a pause – about half the length of the original. This will allow you to give a summarised translation (working first from English into German, and then vice versa). After each pause, one possible way of translating and summarising the statement is presented.

UNIT 8

 PREPARATORY EXERCISE 2

COMBINING AUDIO- AND GROUP-WORK

You are going to hear a number of statements which are of considerable length. However, they contain surprisingly little information. This is how you should approach this exercise:

Step 1   Listen to the description of the scenario.

Step 2   Take a minute to think about what kinds of statements may come up.

Step 3   Now you all listen to the statement and note down a maximum of five points.

Step 4   One of you gives a summarised version in English to the other two, recording what you say.

Step 5   All three of you then discuss this version and consider what has been left out and what should have been included, referring back to the recording if necessary.

Ask yourselves:

> ✔ Would it have been possible to cut out even more?
>
> ✔ Has crucial information been omitted?
>
> ✔ Did the summarised statement preserve the logical structure of the original?

PREPARATORY EXERCISE 3 (GROUP-WORK)

Now it is your turn to be similarly long-winded. For this exercise you should also work in threes.

The sequence is similar to the previous exercise:

Step 1   Each of you chooses one of the topics and scenarios below and then spends some time jotting down a maximum of five ideas or concepts in English which spring to mind in connection with them.

Step 2   Each delivers a long-winded statement to the two others – building in repetitions, stating the same point in different ways, spinning out statements with rhetorical flourishes, etc.

Step 3   One of the other two interprets and summarises the statement.

Step 4   All of you discuss to what extent the person who has made the presentation has been adequately represented by his/her interpreter. Apply the same criteria as suggested above.

Work around some of the following scenarios:

1	A social worker talks about the dangers which watching television presents to children.
2	A teacher talks about the need for regular homework.
3	A businessperson talks about the fact that the education which young people receive in schools does not equip them for the world of work.
4	A client in a travel agency complains that the weather in Gran Canaria was not what he was told it would be at Christmas.
5	A football supporter talks about his love for the sport.
6	A patient complains about the length of time s/he has to wait to be seen by a doctor in hospital.
7	A probation officer argues that putting people into prison is not an efficient way of fighting crime.

UNIT 8

 **DIALOGUE I**

This is a conversation between Tony Mackenzie from the SNP (Scottish National Party) and Peter Mergentheimer who works with the Assembly of European Regions (AER) or as it is referred to in German, **die Versammlung der Regionen Europas (VRE)**. They have met in connection with a conference to discuss the development of devolution in Scotland. The SNP welcomes devolution as it has been introduced in Wales and particularly Scotland, but sees this merely as a step on the road to independence. Herr Mergentheimer is a firm believer in the system of federalism but does not agree with the secessionist tendencies of the SNP. The meeting takes place in Strasbourg, France.

CLASSWORK WITH DIALOGUE I

You will not be asked to translate this dialogue in the first instance, but to listen to the individual interventions taking notes in the source language. Then you will be asked to give a summarised version in the original language i.e. you are not providing a translation but only a summary in the same language. Either record a full version of your source-language summary in class, or do this as an additional follow-up exercise. Follow-up Exercise 2 will give you an opportunity to compare this with our suggested version.

NOTES ON DIALOGUE I

long-standing experience: **eine lange Erfahrung haben, was Föderalismus angeht** would be fine here. Alternatively, **lange** or **langjährige Erfahrung** is a good way to express the extent of the duration.

durchaus: note that this word can be a good way of giving emphasis to agreement or disagreement.

Die Machtkonzentration: 'The concentration of power (in one hand)' – this refers both to the centralisation of power in fewer hands and to the **Gleichschaltung** i.e. the standardisation of the entire structure of society under National Socialism (in English this is often referred to as 'coordination').

devolution: this word has made its way into the German language. An alternative would be **die regionale Selbstverwaltung**. This would have been one of the terms you would be expected to anticipate.

to come to power: **an die Macht kommen** – you could also approach the intervention from a different angle and simply say **nachdem Labour die Wahlen gewonnen hat**.

devolved governments: the easiest solution is to replace 'devolved governments' with the concept of 'devolution' itself and use the translation suggested for this previously.

electorate: simply **die Wähler** or **die Wählerschaft**.

kein/keiner Befürworterin: 'I am not for', or better, 'not in favour of' – a high register rendering might be 'I do not advocate'.

die Zersplitterung: from **der Splitter**, 'splinter' or 'shard' – as a rule the prefix indicates destruction, coming apart. This might be translated as 'fragmentation'.

das Verhältniswahlrecht: 'proportional representation' – as opposed to the British first-past-the-post system.

tartan tax: here we get a clear indication that a speaker knows about a foreign concept. This will allow you to use the English term in the following conversation.

in Ihrem Sinne sein: this is another way of asking if you are in favour of this, or if it meets with your agreement.

people will know that their vote counts: the literal equivalent of the German **ihre Stimme zählt**, another easier way of saying this would be **ihre Stimme ist wirklich wichtig**.

Steuer erheben: 'to raise taxes' – a term which you will probably have anticipated.

die Benachteiligung: this comes from **Nachteil** as opposed to **Vorteil**. The suffix **be** indicates that something is being done to somebody, i.e. somebody is being disadvantaged.

council tax: **die Kommunalsteuer**.

sich einer Meinung anschliessen: 'to share an opinion'.

UNIT 8

 ## FOLLOW-UP EXERCISE 1 FOR DIALOGUE 1

Once you have worked your way through this dialogue by summarising it in the source language, work with it in the usual way. Note that the recording of the dialogue leaves relatively short gaps, so do not be tempted to reproduce redundancies. Record your interpretation. When listening to yourself, ask the following questions: have the crucial points come across clearly, concisely, and convincingly, or have you significantly altered the course of the conversation with your summary?

 ## FOLLOW-UP EXERCISE 2 FOR DIALOGUE 1

You will now hear the same dialogue again. However, this time the formulations will be considerably more succinct. Of course, there is no hard and fast rule about every detail to be left out or retained. Nevertheless this reduced version will give you a reasonable indication of a possible summarised version.

Work with this in the usual manner. Listen to the statement and then record your interpretation in the gap provided. Listen to yourself.

 ## FOLLOW-UP EXERCISE 3 FOR DIALOGUE 1 (PAIR-WORK)

Working in pairs, compare your own abbreviated version with the one prepared by us. Swap between your recordings half way though i.e. at the point where Herr Mergentheimer says: **Da würde ich Ihnen widersprechen**. Have you been too concise, too redundant? If your choices are very different from ours what have they been motivated by, i.e. on what did you base your decision to leave certain things out? Remember the version provided on tape is only one of a multitude of ways of putting things. Also note that it allows for the kind of redundancy which is the hallmark of free, spontaneous speech. However, in terms of the information provided it does convey the main points.

FLEXIBILITY

Skills covered in this unit:

■ **Finding syntactical alternatives for expressing a statement**

■ **Paraphrasing complex statements with basic vocabulary**

Activities include:

■ **Four preparatory exercises. In Preparatory Exercises 1 and 2 (both individual audio-work) you will be asked to express a sentence with different syntactical constructions. In Preparatory Exercises 3 and 4 (pair-work) you will be required to rephrase culturally specific concepts and idioms in simple German**

■ **A dialogue**

ALTERNATIVE PHRASING

When you are interpreting the dialogues in this book you will occasionally find that you simply cannot think of the most appropriate word or phrase for the idea you are trying to express. Whereas translators can pause to think or even look up the word in a dictionary, interpreters have to think on their feet and express the idea as best they can. A certain mental and verbal agility is called for here – and also a willingness to make do with a second-best solution on occasions. It can be useful – both in English and in German – to practise rephrasing ideas using different words and/or constructions. It is important not to end up in a linguistic cul-de-sac simply because you can only think of one way to express an idea!

Take, for example the following statement – which occurs in this unit's dialogue:

> I am the Conservative Party's spokesperson on European affairs.

The appropriate German word for spokesman is **Sprecher**. But what if you don't know this, or the word escapes you in the heat of the moment? How else could you express the idea in English?

How about:

> I represent the Conservative Party on European affairs.
>
> or: I am the representative of the Conservative Party on European affairs.
>
> or: I speak on behalf of the Conservative Party where European affairs are concerned.

None of these formulations is as good as the original – but all of them put across the idea adequately. The same goes for the following alternatives in German:

> Ideal rendering:
>
> Ich bin Sprecher der Konservativen Partei für europäische Angelegenheiten.
>
> Adequate alternative:
>
> Ich vertrete die Konservative Partei in europäischen Angelegenheiten.
>
> or: Ich spreche für die Konservative Partei wenn es um europäischen Angelegenheiten geht.

NB: the two alternatives given above are not ideal, but they are better than starting off **Ich bin einer der ...** and then getting stuck!

When explaining a culturally specific concept, bear in mind who your listener is and what degree of familiarity with the foreign culture you would expect that person to have. The European correspondent of a newspaper is likely to know more about the last German elections than the publicity manager of a football team.

If you find that you have to restart your sentence with a new syntactical construction you should at least attempt to do so without drawing too much attention to this. So do not say to your listeners, 'Sorry, I'll have to start that differently', but restart by saying 'Or rather . . .'. In German you would recommence a sentence with **Beziehungsweise . . .** and follow this with your new version.

PREPARATORY EXERCISE I

Try expressing the following ideas in English using the words or phrases in brackets instead of the original formulation.

1 These countries have the necessary democratic institutions up and running.

   (. . . set up)
   (. . . been introduced)
   (. . . exist)

2 We are in favour of admitting certain countries to the EU.

   (in favour . . . admission)
   (in favour . . . becoming members)
   (think . . . allowed to join)

3 Romania still has a long way to go in terms of the economy.

   (economy . . . make progress)
   (economy . . . underdeveloped)
   (economy . . . lags behind)

4 There is a need for the EU to put its own house in order first.

   (solve . . . problems)
   (concentrate on . . . affairs)
   (focus on . . . internal)

UNIT 9 ....● General Notes

HANDOUT 9.5

ALTERNATIVE CONSTRUCTIONS

You will have noted that reformulation sometimes involves using a completely different construction:

Original	We are in favour of the admission of certain countries to the EU.
Reformulation	We are in favour of certain countries becoming members of the EU.
or	We think certain countries should be allowed to join the EU.

This is well worth practising, particularly in German, where the grammatical endings and word order often change from one phrase to another.

Try formulating the following ideas in German, using the phrases contained in the brackets:

Example:	Hungary is likely to be amongst the front-runners of new countries joining the EU.
	(zu den ersten zählen . . . beitreten)
	Ungarn wird zu den ersten Ländern zählen, die der EU beitreten.
	(eines der ersten . . . Mitglied werden)
	Ungarn wird eines der ersten Länder sein, die Mitglied der EU werden.

PREPARATORY EXERCISE 2

Now try to interpret the following examples with the syntactical constructions suggested. You will hear the English sentence first, then you will be given three different phrases for interpreting this. After each suggestion there will be a pause for your recording. When you start working with the audio, do not worry if your formulation is not exactly the same as the model given after the pause. It is nevertheless good practice to repeat the model sentence during the second pause.

a   These countries have the necessary democratic institutions up and running.

    (haben bereits)
    (existieren bereits)
    (verfügen über)

b   These economic problems urgently need to be solved.

    (dringend gelöst)
    (Lösung notwendig)
    (man muss . . . lösen)

c   The situation in these countries will gradually improve.

    (sich verbessern)
    (mit der Zeit . . . besser werden)
    (früher oder später . . . Verbesserung geben)

d   We also need to reconsider the whole question of the decision-making processes in Brussels.

    (Entscheidungsprozesse . . . neu überdenken)
    (überlegen . . . neue Entscheidungsprozesse brauchen)
    (sich neu überlegen . . . wie man Entscheidungen macht)

PREPARATORY EXERCISE 3 (PAIR-WORK)

Assume that you do not know the correct term for these concepts (in some cases there is no equivalent phrase), and consider how you would paraphrase them in such a way that a German speaker would recognise them and (probably) prompt you with the right word or phrase. It may help to consider how you would rephrase the sentences in English first.

1 More and more British cities are introducing *traffic-calming measures*.

2 The Scots are very enthusiastic about *devolution*.

3 I hope to undertake a *postgraduate research degree* when I have finished my course here.

4 In recent years there have been many cases of *road rage* in Britain.

5 I have decided to *upgrade* my software.

6 Our town recently installed a *water treatment plant*.

7 Modern politicians tend to speak in *soundbites*.

8 Banks in countries like Switzerland are often used by drug smugglers for *money laundering*.

PREPARATORY EXERCISE 4 (PAIR-WORK)

Work in pairs, as for Preparatory Exercise 3. It may be useful to discuss the meaning of each of the following idioms in English first, before attempting to put the point across in German.

1   I wish you would stop *beating about the bush*.

2   We have decided to *turn a blind eye* to the fact that this candidate has not got the right qualifications for the job.

3   I'm afraid that decision of yours has really *landed us in the soup*.

4   We want to *have a level playing field* in these negotiations.

5   We mustn't *try to run before we can walk*.

6   I think we should be careful about these proposed changes in our plan. There is a danger of *throwing the baby out with the bath water*.

7   We must be careful about how we handle this problem – *we're on a very sticky wicket here*.

8   Frankly, by wanting to reduce working hours and get a wage increase at the same time, you're trying to *have your cake and eat it*.

🎧 DIALOGUE I

This is a conversation between Geoffrey Trouthook, one of the Conservative Party's spokespeople on European affairs, and Martin Fischer, SPD member of the Bundestag. The English speaker is keen to find out the opinion of his German colleague on the issue of enlargement of the EU. Their respective positions on the subject will emerge as the conversation develops. What might you expect them to be?

In this dialogue both speakers will come out with a number of rather idiomatic or metaphorical phrases which may appear to pose a problem for any interpreter. Stay cool and remember that it is your job to put across the gist of what is being said. Try to home in on the core meaning of the phrases concerned – and put that across as best you can. You cannot be expected to know the optimum translation for every idiom!

NOTES ON DIALOGUE 1

ganz meinerseits: a useful phrase in response to formal statements of pleasure! 'The pleasure is entirely mine'.

durchaus nicht: **Durchaus** is an intensifier which you may not be familiar with. It also collocates with words like **möglich, denkbar, machbar**.

Why is that?: in German one has to either repeat the phrase: **Warum legt sie so viel Wert darauf?** or say **Warum ist das der Fall?**

die Tschechische Republik: the Germans also sometimes refer to **Tschechien**, whereas in English one always says 'the Czech Republic'. (But **Slovakien** = 'Slovakia').

eine leistungsfähige Wirtschaft: **leistungsfähig** is a much-used word in German. Its translation depends very much on context. Here 'strong' is probably best. But consider: **ein leistungsfähiger Motor** = 'a powerful engine', **ein leistungsfähiges System** = 'a well-functioning system'.

Which particular ones are you thinking of?: **an welche denken Sie insbesondere?** But the simple phrase **Welche, zum Beispiel?** would be just as effective.

solide: if referring to a person 'reliable'. Here, perhaps 'sound'.

GAP: **Gemeinsame Agrarpolitik**.

decision-making processes: this can be translated literally as **Entscheidungsprozesse**. But of course it would also be perfectly adequate to say . . . **die Art und Weise wie Entscheidungen in Brüssel getroffen werden**.

triftige geopolitische Gründe: *triftig* = 'convincing', but here 'good' would do.

Gängelung: 'spoon-feeding'.

Allianzen eingehen: 'to enter into alliances' – a useful collocation to note.

gleichzuschliessen: this should not be a problem – the next sentence makes everything clear!

instability: **Probleme** would solve the problem. **Die Instabilität** would be an alternative.

das Allheilmittel: 'Panacea' is not the only possibility, 'a solution to all one's problems' is just as good.

UNIT 10 ·· ● Introduction

STRUCTURING

Skills covered in this unit:

■ **Recognising structuring devices in a statement**

■ **Recognising structure where this is only implicit i.e. not marked by specific turns of phrase**

■ **Clarifying structure in the interpretation process**

Activities include:

■ **Three preparatory exercises:**

In Preparatory Exercises 1 and 2 you will be asked to work on your own, replacing or creating links between statements. Preparatory Exercise 3 consists of pair work. In this you will practise the structuring of statements.

The dialogue has three parts to it which are increasingly less well or clearly structured. A follow-up exercise is associated with each of these parts. Two of these require you to work with the audio on your own and Follow-up Exercise 3 is pair work.

UNIT 10 ....● General Notes

STRUCTURING DEVICES

We generally find it easier to follow a well-structured argument. This structuring can take the form of an indication that a new topic is being broached, that a speaker is returning to something they have said earlier on, or that s/he is illustrating something by an example. A turn of phrase can indicate that they will now digress, summarise, give a reason, contend a point, etc. In addition, when constructing an argument speakers often indicate the twists and turns of this by saying such things as **einerseits . . . andererseits**. Indeed, one important difference between speakers is the degree to which they are explicit about the structuring of their statements.

The same holds true for different types of conversation. A spontaneous exchange about tuition fees between two students might not be as well-structured as an argument put forward in a debate or as part of a negotiation. It is very important to recognise immediately these logical links, whether they are more elaborate or whether they take the form of conjunctions such as e.g. **aber, weil**.

We have worked with some relevant expressions in this context in Level 1, Units 2 and 6. These will be helpful with your interpretation. Handout 10.3 provides a list of some more commonly used linkwords. It is by no means exhaustive and you should build a glossary of such expressions that provide and strengthen the logical backbone of a statement. Make sure you are also familiar with the English equivalents of these linkwords and phrases.

Linkwords	*More elaborate structuring devices*
'but'	ich muss hier einen Einwand machen
etwas einwenden Jedoch Aber	
'nevertheless'	er muss aber dennoch daruf hinweisen, dass
Dennoch Nichtsdestoweniger Trotzdem	
'because'	Als Grund hierfür nennt er (das Klima)
Aus diesem Grund Daher Weil	
'furthermore'	Folgendes möchte er hinzufügen
Darüberhinaus Und . . . auch Zudem	
'on one hand . . . on the other'	Man muss hier zwei Seiten in Betracht ziehen
zwar . . . aber einerseits . . . andererseits auf der einen Seite . . . auf der anderen Seite	
'if'	Das geht nur unter der Bedingung, dass
Wenn Falls Angenommen	

UNIT 10 ● General Notes

STRUCTURING PHRASES

There are also further structuring devices which speakers use to indicate their communicative intentions. We have come across ways of starting and finishing a conversation before. Now we will introduce some of the more complex ways of doing so:

Speakers may indicate the fact that they want to:

- come back to a topic later in the conversation:

    auf ein Thema später zurückkommen

- preamble their statements with a remark:

    etwas vorwegnehmen

- change the topic of conversation:

    das Thema wechseln

- digress:

    vom Thema abweichen

- ask additional questions:

    in diesem Zusammenhang eine Frage stellen
    eine Frage stellen, die in Verbindung steht mit

- or they may structure interventions in the following manner:

    initially, by way of introduction, firstly
    zunächst, zuerst, als erstes, einleitend

    Afterwards, following this, my next point
    anschliessend, der nächste Punkt ist

    finally, in conclusion
    abschliessend, als letztes will ich darauf hinweisen, dass

- they may indicate an aside:

    to mention in passing
    nebenbei/beiläufig möchte ich darauf hinweisen

IMPLICIT STRUCTURE

Unfortunately, speakers are not always as explicit about the way in which they construct their arguments as we would wish them to be. Their interventions might be well thought out, and points might progress logically from each other, yet this is not necessarily made clear by such linguistic means as we have indicated earlier. In such cases it is often a good idea to impose a structure on the original intervention, if this would make it easier to understand.

Structuring a statement is always an attempt to achieve clarity. A point which merits particular attention here are demonstrative pronouns such as **dies**, **das**, **es**, **sie**, **er**. These can stand in for a word or a concept which has been named before. In this way they provide a very useful shorthand. However, it is very important to make sure that your listener is left in no doubt about what exactly it is they refer to. Consider the following example:

> Umweltschützer kritisieren die Bundesregierung, weil ihre Gesetzgebung nicht der Abfallvermeidung dient. Diese ist der Wiederverwertung bei weitem vorzuziehen.

Here **diese** refers back to the **Abfallvermeidung**, and the words are close enough together to leave no doubt about what the demonstrative pronoun stands in for.

Compare this with the next set of statements:

> Umweltschützer kritisieren die Bundesregierung, weil ihre Gesetzgebung nicht der Abfallvermeidung sondern der Wiederverwertung dient. Damit wird nur ein geringer Prozentsatz an Energie eingespart. Deshalb ist diese die bessere, da ökologischere Lösung des Problems.

Here **diese** is too far removed from **Abfallvermeidung**. The listeners would have to ask themselves which of the two concepts is meant. Of course, this can be reconstructed logically, but the formulation does certainly not make for easy understanding and is even open to misunderstanding.

The same observations apply to instances where you have a delay factor i.e. where speakers finish a statement by saying e.g. 'Am I right in assuming that you support devolution?' And the answer is **Ja das stimmt**. Here your translation should be: 'Yes I do support devolution' rather than 'Yes, that's right', simply because it also functions as a reminder for the listener of what has after all been said three utterances ago.

UNIT 10

 PREPARATORY EXERCISE 1

ADDING LINKS

You will hear a series of two statements in English. Interpret them and connect them with the appropriate linkword in the gap left on the audio. Note that more than one solution might be possible. Listen to yourself to see whether the logical connection is convincing.

You will then hear a series of similar statements, this time, in German. Interpret them, again connecting the two statements with an appropriate linkword.

UNIT 10 ·· ● Activity

🎧 **PREPARATORY EXERCISE 2**

ILLOGICAL OR MISSING LINKS

You will hear some statements in English. These are connected by links which have little logical justification. Listen to these statements then repeat them in English this time with a link which does make sense. The second time round provide a translation into German – again, with the right link. Remember to use the third person.

UNIT 10 ⋯⋯⋯⋯⋯⋯⋯⋯⋯⋯⋯⋯⋯⋯⋯⋯⋯⋯⋯⋯⋯⋯⋯⋯⋯⋯ ● Activity

PREPARATORY EXERCISE 3 (PAIR-WORK)

GIVING A WELL-STRUCTURED STATEMENT

Work in twos. You should each construct a brief outline for a talk on British membership of the European Union – which you advocate as beneficial. The following structuring devices should be employed. Of course you can use others too, but you should definitely incorporate the ones given underneath. Give your brief talks (3 minutes at least) in turn, pausing half-way to give your partner time to interpret into German.

> Initially, I would like . . . Emphasise three advantages . . . firstly, secondly, thirdly. Furthermore I would like to note . . . On the one hand . . . on the other hand . . . Only if . . . For that reason . . . Draw the conclusion Finally return to.

Now do the same, but in German with interpretation into English.

Have structuring devices been well used i.e. if you have said that you will give a reason have you actually done so? Could you have used better, more links?

Now you are asked to produce a similarly well and explicitly structured explanation of the following topics. Start off by doing this in English then give a German version along the same lines. As always a search on the Internet can help with relevant material.

> 1   The financial difficulties of university students. You think that the state should subsidise them more.
>
> 2   Women's emancipation – your argument is that some progress has been made, but on the whole the degree of discrimination is still shocking.
>
> 3   Drug abuse – you maintain that there is a need to differentiate between types of drugs and that some drugs should be legalised.
>
> 4   The media – the invasion of privacy through the media can only be stopped if the public's right to information is violated. This is unacceptable.

🎧 DIALOGUE 1

The following dialogue is subdivided into three parts and will place different types of demands on the interpreter. The first part is clearly and explicitly structured. To interpret this successfully you will have to be familiar with the equivalent turns of phrase in both languages. The second part presents a well-structured argument without necessarily spelling this out as clearly as is the case in Part 1. Here you must add some explicit structure. The third part is badly structured. You should feel free to change the sequence of statements, impose more structure, but also to ask back to elicit the connections between individual statements or even clear up apparent contradictions.

The speakers in this dialogue are Elaine Nowell-Burch, a *Guardian* journalist, and Sigrid Brandt, a former leading executive of the Treuhandanstalt (THA). Frau Brandt is a member of the CDU, the party which was in power while German reunification came about. During her time at the Treuhand, Frau Brandt has frequently come under criticism for the tough stance on privatisation in the former GDR which she had pushed for. You should familiarise yourself with the shortcomings which have been blamed on the THA.

UNIT 10 .... ● Vocabulary

NOTES ON DIALOGUE I

PART I

to tape: this should have been anticipated – **auf Band aufnehmen**.

die Einschränkung: 'to make a reservation'.

publication: again, an item to be prepared for: **die Veröffentlichung (in)**.

to do a good job: **gute Arbeit leisten**.

criticism directed at: the collocation is **Kritik üben an etwas jemandem**.

gehen wir doch so vor: 'let's discuss points in this order'.

konsequent: a favourite German word, meaning 'consistent(ly)'.

Firmen in staatlichem Besitz: another prime candidate for anticipation: 'state-owned enterprises'.

abhängig von etwas: 'dependent on'.

subsidy: **die Subvention**.

PART 2

average income: **das Durchschnittseinkommen**.

unrealistische Erwartungen: 'expectations were too high'.

die Volkswirtschaft: 'the economy'.

zusammenbrechen: in the context, 'the markets had collapsed'.

to save from privatisation: **die Privatisierung hätte verhindert werden können**.

in a better condition: **in besserem Zustand**.

too little too late: quite literally – **zu wenig und zu spät**.

PART 3

the condition: in this context **Konditionen** (i.e. of a contract) is appropriate.

die Arbeitsplatzzusage: 'a pledge to create jobs', Frau Brandt provides another translation in her next intervention.

der Vertrag: 'contract'.

a Western-style economy: this requires paraphrasing e.g. **ein Wirtschaftssystem nach westlichem Modell**, though less elegant but acceptable is **ein Wirtschaftssystem wie im Westen**.

von rationalen Überlegungen geleitet: 'led by rational considerations'.

FOLLOW-UP EXERCISE 1

Listen to Part 1 of the dialogue. Stop the audio after each intervention. Give a rendering in the source language. When listening to this ask yourself whether you have made good use of the very clear structure provided by the speaker. Have you interpreted them throughout with the appropriate terminology?

FOLLOW-UP EXERCISE 2

Listen to Part 2 of the dialogue. Stop the audio after each intervention and ask yourself whether it might be helpful to a listener if your interpreted version would provide a much more clear structure. With some interventions this will be the case but with others you will be able to do a straightforward interpretation. Listen to your recorded version asking yourself whether your interpretation does improve the clarity of what has been said.

FOLLOW-UP EXERCISE 3 (PAIR-WORK)

Working in pairs, listen to Part 3 of the dialogue. Stop the audio after each intervention. Reformulate each intervention into something more structured and easy to understand. Record your version and exchange this with your partner. Working from this restructured version you should interpret the dialogue. Discuss your solutions for the reformulations and the interpretation with your partner.

UNIT 11

ANTICIPATION

Skills covered in this unit:

■ **Anticipating statements on the basis of prior information about the speakers and the general context of the dialogue**

■ **Anticipating the continuation of a statement on the level of the sentence**

Activities include:

■ **Two preparatory exercises: Preparatory Exercise 1 will ask you to anticipate the content and attitude of speakers' statements. Preparatory Exercise 2 will require you to anticipate the continuation of a statement**

■ **One dialogue in two versions. The first is gapped and you will be asked to anticipate these omissions. The second provides a full rendering of the statements**

EXPECTATIONS AS A LISTENER

In all conversations the speakers – unless they are extremely bored or distracted – tend to listen actively to each other, building up certain expectations on the basis of what the other person has already said or is in the process of saying. If they know each other's attitude to the subject under discussion, they probably have certain expectations even before the conversation has started! It is essential that the interpreter – who, after all, has to translate all these statements into another language – should also approach his/her job actively and try to anticipate their content. Anticipation can take many forms, but it is helpful to distinguish two general kinds:

> 1   Anticipation at macro level – building up expectations as to a person's line of argument and his or her partner's response.
>
> 2   Anticipation at micro-level – predicting, at the level of the sentence, what is going to come next.

The value of 1 should be obvious. If an interpreter has a reasonably clear idea of the sort of line of argument his or her customers are going to take, then s/he can anticipate what terms are liable to crop up and prepare accordingly. Not only that, but when it actually comes to interpreting the speaker's statements, it is much easier to process these and concentrate on how to formulate them if you have – at least to some extent – been able to anticipate their content. If everything a speaker says comes as a surprise to the interpreter, then it is very easy to suffer from information overload and break down under the strain. On the other hand, if the interpreter is familiar with the subject matter and the attitudes of the speakers then s/he can sit back and enjoy the job!

If it is a discussion:

> What issues are likely to arise?
> What will their attitude be?
> Will they tend to agree on certain things, or will they end up disagreeing on virtually everything?
> What arguments are they likely to put forward to support their case?

If it is an interview:

> What questions is the interviewer likely to ask?
> What will the reaction of the interviewee be?
> Will there be any questions s/he will refuse to answer?

continued

UNIT 11 ······································● General Notes

If it is a negotiating session:

> What will each of the speakers be trying to achieve?
> How will they do this – what arguments will they use?
> Are they likely to give way on any matters?
> What will their priorities be?

Once you have worked out possible answers to some of the above questions, you should consider what sort of language will be involved. What terms are likely to come up? What set phrases or formulations? Try to build up a list – not just of individual words, though there may be a few key terms which you will need – but also of verbal phrases:

> Massnahmen ergreifen
> einen Punkt anschneiden
> einen Kompromiss schliessen, etc.

ANTICIPATION OF SPEECH ACTS

Another aspect of anticipation relates to the speech acts that are likely to occur:

In a discussion, expressions of agreement and disagreement are bound to crop up such as 'I can't agree with you there', 'I must say I agree with you'.

In an interview, the interviewer will express his/her gratitude and will probably also use structuring phrases like 'Can I ask you a different question?' or 'Can I come back to something you said before?'

In negotiations, expressions of approval and disapproval will be used: 'We find that perfectly acceptable' or 'I'm afraid we cannot accept that'. And proposals will be made such as 'May I suggest the following', and demands expressed like 'We insist that you accept this'.

ANTICIPATION AT THE LEVEL OF THE SENTENCE

Even at sentence level it is often possible to predict what is going to come next. If one speaker has made a suggestion and the other one starts off:

> Es tut mir leid, aber . . .

Then you can be pretty sure that what is going to follow is a rejection of the suggestion!

Or if a speaker has claimed that his or her company has taken a number of measures and then says:

> Lassen Sie mich Ihnen . . .

It is likely that what follows is:

> . . . ein Beispiel nennen or geben.

As often as not, one can also anticipate on the basis of linguistic collocations. Thus if a politician starts a sentence:

> Was die Beschäftigungspolitik anbetrifft, so haben wir eine Reihe von Massnahmen . . .

continued

UNIT 11

General Notes

There is a fair chance the verb is going to be **ergriffen** or **eingeführt**, because these are both verbs that collocate or combine with **Massnahmen**.

Thinking ahead even within a single statement ensures that you remain alert and makes it easier for you to take notes. You are less likely to have to ask back because you did not hear a particular word and you are also less likely to distort the logic of what you are interpreting.

UNIT 11

Your ability to anticipate statements and attitudes will be fine-tuned during any extended conversation. This is especially the case in conversations where speakers represent a certain opinion or interest. The same applies with regard to the way in which they speak i.e. do they tend to be long-winded or succinct, do they structure statements clearly or is the logical structure of what they say difficult to follow?

PREPARATORY EXERCISE 1

The dialogue for this unit consists of a conversation between an American representative of the automotive industry and a German Greenpeace representative during a conference on climate change. Start by jotting down some preparatory notes based on the following points:

AMERICAN INDUSTRIALIST

What might his arguments be?

case against the car unproven	many jobs depend on car industry
global warming can have many causes	unfair to deny the third world the chance to develop
steps are already being taken	

Useful phrases:

Schritte unternehmen	Beweise erbringen
Massnahmen ergreifen	Globale Erwärmung bekämpfen
Emissionen um x% reduzieren	Arbeitsplätze verlieren
dem Treibhauseffekt entgegenwirken	auf etwas zurückzuführen sein

GREENPEACE REPRESENTATIVE

What is the Greenpeace line on climate change?

How might he respond to the above arguments?

plenty of proof available	alternative jobs must be found
the car is a major cause of global warming	third world must avoid our mistakes
steps already taken do not go far enough	

Useful phrases:

es ist erwiesen worden, dass	alternative Beschäftigungsmöglichkeiten finden
nicht weit genug gehen	die Fehler der Industrienationen vermeiden

Now record a short English and German brief such as might be given to an interpreter before s/he starts the assignment.

🎧 PREPARATORY EXERCISE 2

This exercise offers you a chance to try your hand at intelligent anticipation.

Listen to the dialogue. Every now and then the speakers will stop in mid-sentence. Stop the audio and consider, on the basis of what has gone before and what you know about their attitudes, how they might have finished the sentence, then press 'start' again and listen to what was actually said! Obviously it is unlikely that you will always be able to predict exactly how the speaker was going to finish the sentence, but you will be surprised by how often you can work out the general direction the statement was moving in.

If your prediction is well clear of the mark, take a moment or two to consider why this was the case. Did you not pick up certain indicators in the context? Or maybe things were not as unambiguous as you might have thought.

UNIT 11

 DIALOGUE 1

Once you have completed Preparatory Exercise 2 (Handout 11.6) try doing the full dialogue as a normal liaison interpreting exercise. You will have realised by now that any specialist terms are confined to 'global warming', 'emissions', and 'carbon dioxide'.

Please note two things:

✓ This dialogue offers you considerable scope for taking the sort of flexible approach to expressing ideas which you practised in Unit 9.

✓ There are also a number of cases where you will need to expand on what one of the speakers has said, because he is reacting to something he has just heard, and the time delay means that additional clarification is required.

NOTES ON DIALOGUE I

Automobilindustrie: the industry often refers to itself in English as the 'automotive industry'. 'Car industry' is, strictly speaking, not precise enough, as it excludes vans and lorries.

predictions of global warming: **Vorhersagen/ Prognosen, was die globale Erwärmung anbetrifft.**

has agreed to cut emissions: **. . . hat . . . einer Reduzierung der Emissionen zugestimmt.**

by 6%: **um 6%.**

by the year 2005: **bis zum Jahr 2005.**

appreciate: **verstehen** or **begreifen.**

hundreds of thousands of jobs: ***hunderttausende von Arbeitsplätzen.***

to do without: ***auf etwas verzichten.***

als wild abtun: 'dismiss as wild'.

UNIT 12 ··· ● Introduction

PRESENTATION

Skills covered in this unit:

■ **The use of non-linguistic aspects of interpreting**

■ **To communicate efficiently while interpreting**

Activities include:

■ **Two preparatory exercises:**

> **The first of these will require you to take your cue from a speaker's intonation, and the second to improve on this. The first follow-up exercise will be an assessment of your interpretation of the dialogue. The second follow-up exercise will provide you with an interpreted version of this unit's dialogue. You will be asked to analyse the interpreter's rendering and improve on it.**

■ **A dialogue**

UNIT 12 ● General Notes

NON-LINGUISTIC COMMUNICATION

In the final analysis, liaison interpreting is all about communication. While the verbal aspect is, of course, central to this, here, just as in everyday conversations, there are also other ways in which information is transmitted: facial expressions, gestures, intonation all play an important part in facilitating communication. Often students get so absorbed in the process of interpretation that they forget about these communication tools which they will make ample use of as soon as they leave the classroom. And yet a rendering which is linguistically well-expressed, structured, and concise will fall short of its function if it is not delivered well, i.e. if what comes across is not the intention to communicate a statement but rather hesitation and self doubt; if the intonation is monotonous and does nothing to structure the statement; or even if the interpreter never establishes eye contact with the person s/he is speaking to. In the event a less accurate rendering with more communicative thrust might well be more convincing.

We often have little awareness of our own way of speaking or of our communicative idiosyncrasies. It is therefore important to assess your own delivery by recording and listening to yourself. In some cases this will create an awareness that the delivery has to be more lively. In other cases it might make speakers aware that they need to tone down exaggerated intonation.

In this unit we will provide some pointers to the main pitfalls and give some examples of good, or not so good, practice. Obviously, effective communication is a crucial skill for many types of verbal interaction, be it job interviews, presentations, or teaching.

The following are important points to remember:

ENUNCIATION

Rule number one in this context has to be that you must speak clearly and reasonably loudly. After all you are there to aid understanding and to be understood.

INTONATION

This is an important device with which we do not merely liven up a statement but more crucially structure our interventions e.g. by giving added weight to an adjective, or flagging a statement as a mere aside. As pointed out previously, intonation can also stand in for vocabulary i.e. to indicate how beautiful something is, or, how odious you find a particular policy.

EYE CONTACT

Establish eye contact with the person you talk to. This serves a threefold purpose. The person you talk to is prone to feel rather detached if there is nobody to look at while they are saying something or listening to what is being said. This soon gives a speaker the impression that s/he is speaking into a void. Furthermore, it has been shown that we actually understand better if we scan a speaker's face and in particular lip movements while s/he speaks. Looking at a person can also give you some immediate indication as to whether your message is coming across, since most speakers will give very clear signs of confusion, surprise, approval or disapproval when listening to something which does not make sense to them. Note that this is an aspect that should be borne in mind when doing any form of group- and pair-work.

continued

UNIT 12 ....● General Notes

PACE OF SPEAKING

Students are frequently exposed to situations where they have to assimilate verbally transmitted information. You will thus be aware that some speeds of speaking make it easier or indeed very difficult to allow you to do this. When we speak in a public situation we tend to be nervous. Our natural reaction often is to speak faster.

Speaking more slowly, however, does give us more time to think and more scope for managing our intonation. Could you work from your own renderings, or would they be too fast? Or adversely, do you tend to be so slow as to lose the attention of your listener?

USE OF NOTES

When we speak freely we quite automatically make use of non-verbal means of communication. As soon as notes are involved, we tend to become dependent on the written word and the temptation is to read from notes rather than to speak to somebody. When working with notes make it a principle to look up from the page at irregular intervals. This in turn will give you an indication whether your notes are taken in such a way that allows you to assimilate them with a quick glance, or whether there is simply too much on the page in an impenetrable layout with no differentiation between primary and secondary information.

ENDING A STATEMENT

It is particularly important that speakers are left in no doubt as to whether the interpreter has finished a statement. This makes it clear to them that it is now up to them to take their turn in the conversation. For the student interpreter, ending an intervention in a decisive manner often presents a problem, because it requires the quick decision that what has been said fully reflects the original statement and it is now time to stop. The result can sometimes be fudged endings, redolent of hesitation and an unwillingness to end lest something might have been missed out after all. In this kind of situation the listener wonders about the actual thrust of a statement or when it is appropriate for her or him to respond. Falling intonation, slowing down the speaking pace, re-establishing eye contact are all ways in which we can indicate that we have said our piece and that the ball is now – firmly – in somebody else's court.

POLITENESS STRATEGIES

It has already been mentioned that these differ between languages. And do not forget that the register and degrees of politeness which you produce will colour the listener's view of the person whose thoughts and statements s/he has only indirect access to.

The effect which a good or bad delivery on the part of an interpreter has on their listeners has been studied extensively. The results show that it is this aspect which has a crucial impact on a listener's assessment of the quality of interpreting. After all, the interlocutors might not understand the German or English but they will be able to distinguish a good communicator from a bad one.

UNIT 12

 PREPARATORY EXERCISE 1

The following exercise is designed to jog your intonation. First you will hear a text in German. This is on the topic of increasing poverty in the world and the potential this creates for social and global conflicts. It is delivered with a lot of conviction and the intention to persuade the listener of what is being said. The speaker will pause at intervals and you are asked to repeat the gist of it in German with the same enthusiasm. You will have to take notes for this exercise as individual passages are lengthy. Record yourself and listen to your delivery. Is it convincing? Now listen again and try to do the same in English.

NOTES ON PREPARATORY EXERCISE 1

der Gegensatz: here 'contradictions'.

die Lösung: 'the solution'.

gesamtgesellschaftliche Konsequenzen: 'consequences for all of society'.

auf jemandenletwas angewiesen sein: 'be dependent on'.

die Belastung: 'the burden on'.

bedrohlich: 'threatening'.

der Sozialstaat: 'the welfare state'.

das Entwicklungsland: 'the developing country'.

die Bekämpfung: 'the battle against'.

zu etwas zählen: 'to be amongst'.

die Tatsache: 'the fact'.

verteilt sein: 'to be distributed'.

die Festung Europa: 'Fortress Europe', in English as in German this has come to be a recognised term.

der Rand: here: 'the periphery'.

offensichtlich: 'obvious'.

verhindern: 'to prevent'.

UNIT 12 ....• Activity

 PREPARATORY EXERCISE 2

In the second exercise your English speaker will be quite monotonous, despite the fact that his topic is an emotive one: the work of Unicef in trying to protect the rights and lives of children. Listen to the audio and use the gaps to give an improved delivery. Again, the length of the individual passages requires the taking of some notes. Record yourself. Has your delivery improved on the original version? Now try the same in German.

Note that of course the intention here is not to shadow every change of intonation in a speaker. It is neither desirable to reproduce the tedium of a speaker nor her or his individual way of speaking. The guiding principle here is that you should render a statement in a way which serves the same communicative function it had when it was first made i.e. to convince, to express disagreement, to explain facts, etc.

106

NOTES ON PREPARATORY EXERCISE 2

according to: **nach** (followed by dative).

victim: **das Opfer**.

need: here: **die Bedürftigkeit**.

discrimination: **die Diskriminierung**.

the foundation: **die Gründung**.

need: in this context: **das Bedürfnis**.

to give way: **etwas ist (einer anderen Sache) gewichen**.

the final resort: **letztendlich**.

resolution: **die Resolution, die Erklärung**.

to fill an empty stomach: **einen leeren Magen füllen**.

to implement: **etwas implementieren**.

in the spirit of: **im Geiste** (followed by genitive).

effort: **die Anstrengung**.

basic schooling: **Grundausbildung**.

nutrition: **die Ernährung**.

health care: **die Gesundheitsfürsorge**.

oppression: **die Unterdrückung**.

DIALOGUE 1

This is a conversation between Ms Critchley from the BBC and Herr Thomalla who is one of the programmers of the Television Channel ARTE. ARTE was founded in 1991 and due to its general focus it is sometimes referred to as the European Culture Channel. It broadcasts in several languages and its share of the European television audience is relatively small.

We have recorded two versions of this dialogue. The input from the two speakers is the same in both versions. The first should be interpreted in the usual manner, but particular emphasis should be placed on aspects of delivery as outlined above. Version 2 provides an interpretation of the dialogue which is perfectly acceptable in linguistic terms. However, the unsatisfactory way in which this is rendered illustrates many of the issues outlined above. Analyse the delivery and its faults.

UNIT 12 · ● Vocabulary

NOTES ON DIALOGUE I

Since an interpretation of this dialogue is given on the tape, these notes only suggest a few terms.

the programme: **das Programm**, Germans will also talk about, for example, **das zweite Programm**, meaning 'the second channel', the ZDF.

das Unternehmen: 'the company'.

die Ausstrahlung: 'transmission', 'broadcasting'.

die Finanzierung: 'funding'.

advertising: **die Werbung**.

die öffentlichen Gelder: 'public funding'.

budget: **das Budget**, **der Haushalt**.

private channel: **der Privatkanal**.

konkurrieren mit: 'to compete with'.

das Profil: 'the profile'.

FOLLOW-UP EXERCISE 1

Record your interpretation of this dialogue. Listen to your recording, and assess yourself using the following criteria:

✔ Pace – are you speaking fluently or at a very uneven pace? Do you backtrack a lot?

✔ Speed – are you speaking at a speed that makes it easy to assimilate information?

✔ Intonation – do you use this to emphasise points or do you not use it as a means of differentiating between the general flow of information?

✔ Enunciation – do you speak clearly or do you swallow syllables?

✔ Ending a statement – is this done confidently?

✔ Politeness – do you convey the marked note of politeness between these two speakers?

✔ Eye-contact – have you managed to look up from your notes at regular intervals and at the end of statements or have your eyes been glued to your notes?

🎧 FOLLOW-UP EXERCISE 2

Now listen to the interpreted version of the dialogue. Linguistically, this provides you with a perfectly acceptable translation. However, the delivery requires improvement. Listen to the interpreter's rendering and take notes. After each intervention stop the audio. Analyse the faults of the delivery and improve on it.

Level 3 assumes an advanced degree of proficiency in the understanding and speaking of German and an ability to put statements in the foreign language into succinct and appropriate English.

Before tackling this level:

✓ You will have had an opportunity to practise the skills discussed in Level 2 and developed an awareness of when to use them.

✓ You should have learnt to trust your ability to memorise several chunks of meaning and have developed a way of triggering your memory with a few clearly written notes.

✓ Your delivery should sound convincing to a listener.

✓ You should be aware of the criteria against which to assess your own performance when doing liaison interpreting in class or when listening to a recording.

✓ Most of all, however, you should have reached the point where you never succumb to the temptation to give up: there is always a strategy to get out of a tight spot – by asking back, expressing things more simply, leaving out redundancies or rhetorical flourishes, etc.

The dialogues will be taken from a number of different contexts and will focus on a broad variety of subjects. We have grouped them into three types:

---

1   Exposition – somebody explains something to somebody who has a greater or lesser degree of familiarity with the subject matter, e.g. a journalist questions a politician.

2   Argumentation – two people exchange different views about a topic e.g. a Europhobe and a Europhile discuss the single currency.

3   Negotiation – two people confer with the intent of achieving consensus or a solution to a problem e.g. the sale of a piece of machinery is being discussed between an interested but demanding buyer and a seller who can only make a limited amount of concessions.

Of course, such categories are never absolute – any negotiation, for example, will be likely to require a certain amount of explanation as well. But one of these three elements will predominate in each of the dialogues presented. What we are emphasising by this broad classification is the fact that there are types of conversations which – even though the topic matter differs widely – involve comparable interpreting skills and there is therefore scope for anticipating the problems involved.

There are no exercises associated with the dialogues at Level 3, as it is the dialogues themselves which form the exercises. Before starting the dialogues you should always spend some time considering what is likely to come up on the basis of the information you receive in advance. Your self-study work after class will consist in working with the taped versions of the dialogue. As before, you should aim to do several recordings until you have produced a recorded version which you feel satisfied with in terms of the criteria discussed in Level 2.

continued

AIMS OF LEVEL 3

This book does not provide a foundation for professional interpreter training – if only because, were we to aim for this, we would have to assume that your understanding of the foreign language would be near perfect.

However, once you have successfully worked through Level 3, you should be able to manage a liaison interpreting situation reasonably confidently, provided that:

✓ The statements are of a reasonable length.

✓ The statements are delivered in something not too remote from standard German.

✓ You are given the opportunity to prepare yourself beforehand on the basis of background information.

✓ It is understood that your interpretations into the foreign language will never be faultless and might even require further clarification.

✓ It is understood that you may have to elicit clarification of unknown vocabulary and have to ask for explanation of culturally specific concepts.

UNIT 13

HANDOUT 13.1

EXPOSITION

The first dialogue of Level 3 is of an 'expository' nature. In the way the term is used for our purposes, exposition indicates a situation where we have a clear division of roles i.e. A wants to glean some knowledge or information from B. Typically A will therefore be asking the questions and B providing the answers. It is obviously helpful to know to what extent your questioner is familiar with the topic s/he is asking about, as this will have an influence on the degree of sophistication you can expect in a question. Thus a more knowledgeable speaker will tend to pepper her/his questions with some of their own insights. It is also a pointer as to the amount of explanation that you will have to provide when it comes to culturally specific topics and knowledge.

113

UNIT 13

 DIALOGUE 1 (TOWN PLANNING)

Paul McBryde, a journalist from *The Scotsman*, one of the main Scottish daily newspapers with a nationwide circulation, meets Christa Huber, an official from Munich to hold an interview on the setting up of twinning arrangements between Edinburgh and Munich. Exchange arrangements at secondary school level and for vocational training will be the focus of the discussion. While these have been agreed on in principle, a detailed programme is yet to be drawn up during the course of a series of meetings. While familiarity with a British environment can be presumed for the German speaker, the Scottish journalist has no particular knowledge of Germany.

In addition to the general assessment criteria which apply to this exercise, as you listen to your recording of this dialogue ask yourself:

✔ Are you clear about what exactly Mr McBryde wants to know?

✔ Have you catered for cultural differences?

NOTES ON DIALOGUE I

to tape: **eine Tonbandaufnahme machen, etw. auf Band aufnehmen**.

die Ausstrahlung: 'broadcasting'

der Rektor: 'principal', 'headteacher'.

Azubi: abbreviation for **der/die Auszubildende**, often still referred to by the term **Lehrling**. **Azubi** served to replace **Lehrling** as a more egalitarian term.

to target: **abzielen auf jmd, jmd anpeilen**.

UNIT 14 ∙∙∙∙∙∙∙∙∙∙∙∙∙∙∙∙∙∙∙∙∙∙∙∙∙∙∙∙∙∙∙∙∙∙∙ ● Introduction

NEGOTIATION

The definition of negotiation for the purpose of this book is that it involves discussion aimed at achieving a solution. Typically, but not necessarily three phases can be distinguished here:

> ✔ Setting out the problem and establishing the position of the speakers.
>
> ✔ Identifying areas of agreement and disagreement.
>
> ✔ Discussion of possible solutions.

Interactions of this type can be fraught. Tempers may run high and positions may be intransigent. This begs the question: what is the interpreter's role? Does s/he try to mediate, or merely reproduce expressions of anger and frustration? What amount of control is s/he allowed to assume over the conversation? The general rule here is that the purpose of the exercise is to facilitate communication: if anger is expressed, this is what must be conveyed. (But the interpreter can confine him/herself to expressing this linguistically – body language, intonation, pitch, facial expression, etc., will come across even in a foreign language. In other words, if one of the speakers raises his/her voice and thumps on the table, there is no need for the interpreter to do the same!) However, no negotiation has ever been advanced by mere rudeness (and luckily, negotiations rarely reach this stage of disintegration). The interpreter has the option to convey the function without reproducing the insult. So **Sie lügen ja wie gedruckt** is probably best translated rather more neutrally as 'He considers this statement to be untrue'.

In addition to content based anticipation these dialogues provide scope for anticipating the strategies the speakers will employ, e.g. on which points will they be intransigent and when will they be prepared to compromise? If they do make concessions what are these likely to be and how will they justify them without simply admitting that they are giving in under pressure? How forceful are speakers likely to be in voicing their demands?

🎧 DIALOGUE I (CO-DETERMINATION)

In the course of a drive for lower unit costs and higher productivity, the US parent company of a number of subsidiaries has announced plans to introduce a three-shift working day instead of a two-shift one throughout their plants in Europe. This follows downsizing and thus making staff redundant in a number of European subsidiaries, including the Hanover plant where this conversation takes place: only one year before this discussion the Works Council (**der Betriebsrat**) and unions agreed to accept a programme of redundancies to ensure the financial viability of the plant. The Works Council chairman of the Hanover subsidiary, Herman Schramm (**der Betriebsratvorsitzende**), has been made aware of the plans by management to introduce a three-shift system. He is taking the opportunity to discuss the matter during a visit of the Chief Personnel Officer, Peter Marshland, to Germany. Herr Schramm wants to get further information and register his colleagues' protest at the proposed measures. You cannot assume that Mr Marshland has an in-depth knowledge of the German system of co-determination.

UNIT 14 .... ● Activity

WORKING WITH YOUR RECORDING

In addition to the general assessment criteria which apply to this exercise as you listen to your recording of this dialogue ask yourself:

✓ Has the intention of the original statement been conveyed adequately? (Note that this is conveyed by the choice of words as much as by the tone of voice. The interpreted version should reflect this.)

✓ Have you been sufficiently aware and communicative about cultural differences?

✓ Is your interpretation conducive to conveying the two different kinds of interests around which this conversation revolves i.e. one person wants to sell the other wants to buy?

✓ Have you conveyed the strategies which the speakers use to achieve their aims such as giving assurances, indications of politeness, stating conditions either in a very definitive or a more tentative manner?

✓ When you state what the speaker is doing (i.e. 'He would like to point out to you . . .', 'She has to contradict you on this point . . .') has your introductory statement made it clear what is intended and has this been conveyed with the appropriate force?

NOTES ON DIALOGUE I

das Gerücht: 'rumour'.

workforce: **die Belegschaft**.

overtime: **Überstunden**.

die Unternehmensleitung: 'the management'.

das Betriebsverfassungsgesetz: 'the German Industrial Co-determination Act'.

die Anhörung: 'consultation'.

productivity: **die Produktivität**.

closure: **Stillegung**.

der Personalabbau: 'reduction of jobs' – nowadays more euphemistically referred to as 'downsizing'.

to consult: here: **in die Diskussion einbeziehen, an der Diskussion beteiligt werden**.

to take into account: **in Betracht ziehen**.

(den Betriebsrat) einberufen: 'to assemble/call a meeting (of the Works Council)'.

die Gesprächsbereitschaft: literally: 'preparedness to talk'.

die Verpflichtung: 'obligation'.

UNIT 15

🎧 ARGUMENTATION: DIALOGUE I (PAID AND UNPAID WORK)

Hedmar Kremintzky, a Member of Parliament for Bündnis 90/Die Grünen meets Benjamin Laidlaw from the Office for National Statistics (ONS). This government body has recently published a report. This demonstrates that the functioning of our society is dependent on unpaid domestic work. However, when the economic performance of a country is calculated this is not taken into account. Thus – to use a blatant example – caring for an elderly relative at home is not considered economically productive, whereas selling weapons is. Green and feminist groups in Britain have been pressing for recognition of unpaid labour in the calculation of the economic performance of a country. Frau Kremintzky, who is responsible for economic forecasting and reporting in her party, has asked for a meeting with Mr Laidlaw to gain some insight into the findings of the report. The meeting takes place in London.

In addition to the general assessment criteria which apply to this exercise, as you listen to your recording of this dialogue ask yourself:

> ✓ Have you listened out for what exactly it is that Frau Kremintzky wants to know?
>
> ✓ Have you conveyed the figures accurately?

NOTES ON DIALOGUE 1

die Wirtschaftsleistung: 'economic performance'.

die Hausarbeit: 'domestic work' is probably better here than 'housework'.

the workplace: **der Arbeitsplatz**.

economic activity: here: **bezahlte Arbeit**.

the size of the economy: **die Grösse des volkswirtschaftlichen Aufkommens**.

miteinbezogen: 'taken into consideration'.

professional tradespeople: **Handwerker**.

the manufacturing sector: **der Fertigungssektor, die herstellende Industrie**.

the economy: **die Volkswirtschaft**.

UNIT 16 ·· ● Background Notes

 NEGOTIATION: DIALOGUE I (COMPUTER EQUIPMENT PURCHASE)

Mr Gerard Millar is the Managing Director of a branch of the Europe-wide insurance company Safe and Sound in Birmingham. This branch is about to purchase 200 computers and has put the order out for tender. Having made a selection amongst the offers received, Mr Millar has now arranged a meeting with the German supplier CSP, which his company is most interested in. Two important factors have influenced this choice: the strength of the pound in relation to the euro at the time of negotiations and the fact that CSP has been highly recommended since it has recently supplied equipment to two German branches of the same insurance company.

Mr Millar will want to clarify the following points in particular: the possibility of purchasing peripheral equipment together with the computers, the warranty conditions offered, the delivery time and the question of installation.

Sigrid Blankenfeld represents CSP. Her company is very keen to get a foothold in the British market and she is therefore prepared to compromise on price and conditions. The meeting takes place in Birmingham.

As you listen to your recording ask yourself:

> ✓ Is your interpretation conducive to conveying the two different kinds of interests around which this conversation revolves i.e. one person wants to sell the other wants to buy?
>
> ✓ Have you conveyed the strategies which the speakers use to achieve their aims such as giving assurances, indications of politeness, stating conditions either in a very definitive or a more tentative manner?
>
> ✓ When you state what the speaker is doing (i.e. 'He would like to point out to you . . .', 'She has to contradict you on this point . . .'). Has your introductory statement made it clear what is intended and has this been conveyed with the appropriate amount of forcefulness?

NOTES ON DIALOGUE I

the department: **die Abteilung**.

to recap: **um (es) zusammenzufassen**.

die Lieferfrist: 'the deadline for delivery'.

das Peripheriegerät: 'peripheral equipment'.

up and running: **betriebsbereit sein**.

the costing: **der Kostenvoranschlag**.

warranty conditions: **die Garantieleistung**.

der Aufpreis: 'additional charge' – which has been used previously – could be recycled here, or 'increase in price'.

Lieferkosten ab Werk: 'delivery ex factory'.

die Frachtversicherung: 'freight insurance'.

to suffer losses: **Verluste erleiden**.

UNIT 17

EXPOSITION: DIALOGUE 1 (EDUCATION)

This a conversation between *Spiegel* correspondent, Elfriede Seubert and a representative of the British Department of Education and Employment. Frau Seubert is writing a series of articles on the crisis in British education and in particular wishes to discuss the funding problems of universities and the government's proposal to solve these by introducing compulsory fees. Before you listen to the audio, imagine the sort of line which each of the speakers will take. Clearly the government representative will try to defend the new proposals. The *Spiegel* has a long tradition of left-of-centre campaigning and has gained a reputation for its tough interviewing stance.

What concepts will come up? How are these rendered in German?

NOTES ON DIALOGUE 1

Erziehungswesen: here just: **Bildungssystem** – 'education system'.

Berufsbildung: 'vocational training' – **Bildung**, in compounds is very often 'training' rather than 'education'. Cf. **Fortbildung** – 'further training'.

contribution: **der Beitrag**.

average length of studies: **durchschnittliche Studienzeit**.

social justice: **soziale Gerechtigkeit**.

einkommensschwächere Familien: 'low-income families'.

after graduating: **nachdem sie das Studium abgeschlossen haben**.

inordinate burden: **übermässige Schuldenlast**.

balancing: here: **in Einklang bringen**.

🎧 ARGUMENTATION: DIALOGUE 1 (TRAFFIC PLANNING)

This a discussion between a representative of the Automobile Association (AA) and a German traffic planner who is involved in 'green' traffic planning. The latter is visiting the UK to see what is done here in this field. He has visited the relevant people at the Ministry of Transport, but now wishes to sound out the AA.

Before starting this dialogue you should give some thought to the attitudes which the two speakers are likely to have towards the subject.

126

NOTES ON DIALOGUE 1

traffic planning: **Verkehrsplanung.**

vergleichende Studie: 'comparative study'.

thorough: here – **eingehend.**

Kraftfahrzeugsteuer: 'vehicle tax'.

Strassenbenutzungsgebühren: 'road tolls/road pricing/road use charges'.

the budget: **der (Staats-)haushalt.**

inflation rate: **die Inflationsrate.**

access: **der Zugang.**

Strasseninstandhaltung: 'road maintenance/repair'.

it outstrips the costs: **es übersteigt die Kosten.**

to cut back on (public) spending: **öffentliche Ausgaben kürzen.**

you can't make an omelette without breaking eggs: **wenn gehobelt wird, fallen Späne** is the nearest equivalent. How could you say it in more simple terms?

mobility: **die Mobilität.**

Schadstoffemissionen: 'toxic emissions'.

verursachen Sachschäden: 'damage caused to property'.

environmental impact analysis: **eine Umweltverträglichkeitsprüfung (UVP).**

to quantify something: **etwas quantifizieren.**

die Entsorgung von Kraftfahrzeugen: 'disposal of (old) cars'.

identification: **die Identifizierung.**

umweltbelastend: 'having a negative impact on the environment/polluting'.

old bangers: **alte Schrottkisten.**